Jesus' Parables:
Finding Our God Within

Other Books in the Jung and Spirituality Series

CARL JUNG AND CHRISTIAN SPIRITUALITY
Edited by Robert L. Moore

TRANSFORMING BODY AND SOUL
Therapeutic Wisdom in the Gospel Healing Stories
by Steven A. Galipeau

JUNG AND CHRISTIANITY IN DIALOGUE
Faith, Feminism, and Hermeneutics
Edited by Robert L. Moore
and Daniel J. Meckel

LORD OF THE FOUR QUARTERS
The Mythology of Kingship
by John Weir Perry

THE WEB OF THE UNIVERSE
Jung, the "New Physics," and Human Spirituality
by John Hitchcock

SELF AND LIBERATION
The Jung-Buddhism Dialogue
Edited by Daniel J. Meckel
and Robert L. Moore

THE UNCONSCIOUS CHRISTIAN
Images of God in Dreams
by James A. Hall
Edited by Daniel J. Meckel

INDIVIDUATION AND THE ABSOLUTE
Hegel, Jung, and the Path Toward Wholeness
by Sean M. Kelly

Robert Winterhalter
with George W. Fisk

Jesus' Parables: Finding Our God Within

Paulist Press
New York ◇ Mahwah, N.J.

ACKNOWLEDGMENTS

The Publisher gratefully acknowledges use of the following materials: Poem from the *Door of Dreams* by Jessie B. Rittenhouse. Reprinted by permission of Houghton Mifflin Co. All rights reserved. Excerpts from *The Nag Hammadi Library*, edited by James M. Robinson. Copyright © 1978 by E.J. Brill. Reprinted by permission of HarperCollins Publishers.

Library of Congress Cataloging-in-Publication Data

Winterhalter, Robert, 1936-
    Jesus' parables: finding our God within / written by Robert Winterhalter: edited by George W. Fisk.
        p.   cm.–(Jung and Spirituality series)
    Includes bibliographical references and indexes.
    ISBN 0-8091-3442-X (pbk.)
    1. Jesus Christ–Parables. 2. Jesus Christ–Psychology. 3. Jung, C.G. (Carl Gustav), 1875-1961. I. Fisk, George W., 1920- II. Title. III. Series: Jung and spirituality.
BT375.2.W54   1993
226.8'06–dc20   93-26774
                                                                           CIP

Published by Paulist Press
997 Macarthur Blvd.
Mahwah, N.J. 07430

Printed and bound in the United States of America

Contents

SERIES FOREWORD

The *Jung and Spirituality* series provides a forum for the critical interaction between Jungian psychology and living spiritual traditions. The series serves two important goals.

The first goal is: *To enhance a creative exploration of the contributions and criticisms which Jung's psychology can offer to religion.* Jungian thought has far-reaching implications for the understanding and practice of spirituality. Interest in these implications continues to expand in both Christian and non-Christian religious communities. People are increasingly aware of the depth and insight which a Jungian perspective adds to the human experiences of the sacred. And yet, the use of Jungian psychoanalysis clearly does not eliminate the need for careful philosophical, theological and ethical reflection or for maintaining one's centeredness in a spiritual tradition.

The second goal is: *To bring the creative insights and critical tools of religious studies and practice to bear on Jungian thought.* Many volumes in the Jung and Spirituality series work to define the borders of the Jungian and spiritual traditions, to bring the spiritual dimensions of Jung's work into relief, and to deepen those dimensions. We believe that an important outcome of the Jung-Spirituality dialogue is greater cooperation of psychology and spirituality. Such cooperation will move us ahead in the formation of a post-modern spirituality, equal to the challenges of the twenty-first century.

Robert L. Moore
Series Editor

Daniel J. Meckel
Managing Editor

Introduction

I spoke to the prophets; it was I who multiplied visions,
and through the prophets gave parables.

—Hosea 12:10

I would say that is the basic theme of all mythology—that
there is an invisible plane supporting the visible one.

—Joseph Campbell[1]

THE INNER SIGNIFICANCE OF JESUS' PARABLES

Jesus spoke the parables to lift lives from lesser to higher
planes. The purpose of this volume is to seek to continue that
dynamic impact on human lives. To accomplish this it is important to consider not only what a parable is, but also what it
does. The inner dynamic of Jesus' imagery has more than a
mere literary or aesthetic effect. Indeed, these stories can give
profound healing to the individual soul, releasing greater
health and harmony into everyday life.

People in fields unrelated to Bible study affirm, from their
own experience, the energy which can be unleashed from this
type of simple, yet penetrating story. For example, Dolores
Krieger observes:

> Finding that the psyche has a reality as "real" as that of the
> conscious, rational world, but that it must be understood
> within the context of the metaphor, may provide the open
> sesame to doors that have been little noticed in our age.

1

Once we have learned not to fear the images that may arise
from the representations we have stored in our collective
unconscious, and once we allow ourselves adequate access
to this secreted place, many linkages with our ancient and
common heritage as Man can become discernible."[2]

This applies to Jesus' parables because their images represent the inner life which all people share on a deep level,
although their awareness may be of lesser or greater degree.

Many people assume that the master teacher gained most
of the material for his parables from observing the people and
the geographic setting with which he was familiar. This, however, was only of secondary importance. His primary source was
the imagery he received through meditation. It is possible to
slow down the cycles of one's brain waves and yet remain
awake; doing so, the subconscious imagery which appears in
dreams becomes accessible to the conscious mind. Jesus took
this a step further, going beyond his personal field of awareness
and accessing the archetypal imagery which Carl G. Jung and
other twentieth century psychologists have explored. These
archetypal images and symbols are the nucleus around which
his parables are built. The father rejoicing with the return of his
prodigal son, and the chagrin of the rich fool as he sees his life
ebbing away, are scenes which resonate with our deepest racial
memories. This is why the parables are newly meaningful in
every generation.

Unfortunately, the true dynamic of the parables, as spoken
by Jesus, has been obscured by later gospel writers. As explained
by the late New Testament scholar, Norman Perrin of the
University of Chicago:

> The parables of Jesus were delivered orally; so far as we
> know, Jesus himself *wrote* no single word of them. We are
> therefore dependent upon texts which were written later,
> and which may or may not represent an accurate reminis-
> cence of the parables as Jesus taught them."[3] *yes!*

I totally agree

The parables, as we shall see shortly, have a definite frame
of reference. Yet within the scope of this framework, they have

a perpetual capacity to generate new meaning. To release this flow of new meaning, a reader has to connect with them in an individual way. Norman Perrin called this the *dynamic interaction* between text and interpreter. The modern scholar Walter Wink advances to an even more specific conclusion, believing that *the interpreter must in turn become interpreted by the text* in order for real inner change to occur. Thus we see that interpretation of the parables is always in process; never can we say, "Now we know all that this story is meant to say."

The parables in the gospel of Thomas, in the main, represent an authentic tradition of Jesus' sayings. Thomas, from a literary standpoint, is independent of the four gospels. As an independent and, for the most part, reliable source, it tends to confirm the parables' authenticity as we find them in Matthew, Mark, and Luke. At the same time, Thomas, in some cases, gives substantial, new information as to their literary form. Also, Thomas restores three parables which were previously lost.

Jesus' Parables: Finding Our God Within also utilizes John Dominic Crossan's *Sayings Parallels: A Workbook for the Jesus Tradition.* Where variant texts are a factor, the number of Crossan's applicable parallel is shown in an Index at the end of this book. For example, "The Cloth and Wineskins" is followed by #98, which includes Matthew 9:16-17, Mark 2:21–22, Luke 5:36b-38, and the non-canonical Thomas 47:4.

It needs to be stressed that symbolic interpretation has—or can have—a valid basis beyond our personal opinion. Images and non-verbal symbols have an existence apart from the individual's conscious knowledge and use of them. They also have the capacity to enter into individual psyches below the threshold of conscious mind, i.e. into the right brain hemisphere in most people, which is closely connected with the subconscious. These images then impress themselves upon the left brain hemisphere, which in turn translates them into words.

This process can occur in a variety of ways, such as through dreams, by means of mental pictures seen in meditation, or more systematically through guided imagery as practiced by Ira Progoff and his students. A writer, while under the influence of this collective imagery, will show an interaction between right brain images and left brain language that goes beyond mere conscious intent. While these images can be shared through literary influences and cultural contacts, they are also communicated across time and space by telepathic means alone.

Carl G. Jung coined the term "collective unconscious" to designate this symbolic field. The majority of his readers probably do not accept all his views as correct. Most regard his writings to be not so much a guiding authority as a quarry to be mined. Nevertheless, the core of his work is increasingly being recognized as valid. Jung wrote:

> A more or less superficial layer of the unconscious is undoubtedly personal. I call it the *personal unconscious*. But this personal unconscious rests upon a deeper layer, which does not derive from personal experience and is not a personal acquisition but is inborn. This deeper layer I call the *collective unconscious*. I have chosen the term "collective" because this part of the unconscious is not individual but universal; in contrast to the personal psyche, it has contents and modes of behaviour that are more or less the same everywhere and in all individuals. It is, in other words, identical in all men and thus constitutes a common psychic substrate of a suprapersonal nature which is present in every one of us.[4]

It is, then, a fact that various images and non-verbal symbols kept appearing in biblical writings at different times, in different places, by different authors, often apart from any conscious intent. This is not limited to the Bible, but still occurs widely in the process of literary creation, independently of language, tradition, and other outside influences.

Regarding the parables, however, it is necessary to state the difference between two procedures which, although widely different, appear confusingly similar. The left brain hemisphere can, within limits, construct its own arbitrary symbology and impose it on a passage. This is what happened when Jesus' parables were treated as allegories with only one possible level of meaning. By contrast, many of the mental pictures and non-verbal symbols that move through the right brain hemisphere—and pervade the parables—have archetypal roots. They cannot be made to order, and have a real validity.

Most allegorical interpretations of Jesus' parables have been only arbitrary constructs without roots in the collective unconscious or *noosphere*—to use Teilhard's term—of the human race. Whole brain functioning which includes the collective archetypes is obviously needed. The left hemisphere, with its analytical tools, can do much to evaluate historical influences, but finds itself incompetent to deal with the imagery of the right hemisphere. By contrast, the right hemisphere is the province of archetypes and images, but cannot analyze historical factors in which sequences of events are involved. When both hemispheres are fully active, and in a state of creative interaction, real clarity becomes possible.

Even the best scholars would achieve greater clarity by working from this frame of reference. For example, William Barclay shows a curious ambivalence toward spiritual interpretation. In his fine book, *Introducing the Bible*, he rightly rejects Augustine's allegorizing the parable of the good Samaritan (Luke 10:30–36). Just the same, taking his cue from Origen (*De Principiis* 1:16), he presents his own summary of the symbolic meanings of the creation stories (Genesis 1–2), the fall of Man (Genesis 3), and the temptations of Jesus (Matthew 4:1–11; Luke 4:1–13). In support of this, he notes that in the Hebrew tradition, "They have quite a different way of thinking, and this is the most important and the most difficult point of all. Among the Hebrews in biblical times there were few—perhaps none—who thought, or could think in abstract terms and abstract arguments. *They thought in pictures.*"[5]

We need not conclude that the ancient Hebrews lacked the capacity for reasoned discourse. The division of the ancient Mediterranean world into separate Greek and Semitic realms of thought is, after all, an historian's pipe-dream, now largely discredited. It *is* clear, however, that the Semites—and most of all in the classical Hebrew dialects—focused strongly on right-hemispheric contents in the use of their language. The fact is that they *did* express themselves in lyrical and poetic language, as their scriptures indisputably attest.

Nor are we to think that they "settled for second best" in doing so. There are those who assume that thinking in pictures is a defect to be overcome, so that henceforth we may think only in propositions. This prejudice, however, is based on nineteenth century concepts that ignore the basic structure of the human psyche. Indeed, images and not words form the basic constituent parts of Jesus' parables. This is seen in the fact that the parables can be translated into other languages, and still maintain their vital capacity as vehicles of wholeness and inner renewal.

The parables, then, are open-ended, visual metaphors. It does not follow, however, that they are stories which can mean anything. They have a definite frame of reference with which valid interpretations agree. In his book, *In Parables,* Crossan explores the possibility that life itself is parabolic. *In the same sense, in the world of Jesus' parables the inside and the outside are always parallel.* This is also a basic principle of the modern New Thought movement.

In the allegory of Genesis 1:1–2:3, God declares something, and it is so. Within this text, Genesis 1:26–27 affirms that man (male and female) is created in the image of God. As God the Divine Mind thinks and thereby creates, so we—for better or for worse—share this capacity on an individual level and thereby shape our own existence. The parable form as Jesus used it, *in and of itself,* affirms this basic law of creative consciousness: "As we think, so we experience. As within, so without; as above, so below." Thus, any interpretation that denies or ignores this principle is false.

Of equal importance is the unifying theme and symbol of Jesus' parables: *the kingdom of God.* Jesus' kingdom is a state of consciousness in which God is known to be the only reality: the one presence, one mind, one power that is all. As Bernard Scott affirms in his book, *Jesus, Symbol-Maker for the Kingdom,* the kingdom is reality as whole as opposed to reality as divided. Reality as whole is indeed real, as the parables affirm. On the other hand, reality as divided is illusory, and this the parables reject.

The kingdom, then, affirms the unity of being, the rule of God's omnipresence within and around us. "Are not five sparrows sold for two pennies? And not one of them is forgotten before God" (Luke 12:6). Any interpretation that denies or ignores this basic spiritual truth is false.

The history of parables' research over several generations has been difficult and sometimes discouraging. Dead ends and false directions have beset the long road to clarity. Nevertheless, the symbols which pervade and illuminate Jesus' parables need not remain as a *mirror*, merely reflecting our own beliefs back to us. They can become, for us, a real *window* into the mind of Christ. The language of symbols is real, and can be tapped within the depths of our own being. Ira Progoff, commenting upon his group work—which is one way among others of achieving similar results—reports that when students reach a certain stage of progress:

> Individuals cease to be caught in the web of doctrines and are no longer possessed by the particular form of symbolic experience that has happened to come to them. They are able then to see through the symbols and to reach through them to the reality of the encounter for which symbolic experiences are the vehicles. Symbols then become transparent to them, not because they have analyzed their meaning by one intellectual formula or another, but because they have perceived and appreciated the dimension of depth in the psyche within which the elemental symbols are truly real.[6]

In summary, then, Jesus' basic aim in his parables is not to teach theology or ethics. It is to release a new level of experience within us. As we move beyond old boundaries of thought, we make direct contact with the divine omnipresence and thus with the unitive nature of being. In so doing, our lives are permanently transformed.

Section I—
THE REVOLUTION
WITHIN

The world of Jesus' parables is not to be entered into lightly, for, once entered into, our lives can never be as before. He designed his parables to lift us above the false, shallow patterns or paradigm called "the mind of the flesh." The images from the Nazarene usher us into the "Mind of the Spirit." This revolution of consciousness transforms our inner world, and with it our outer experience; for in the world of parables, the inner and the outer are always parallel. Divine Mind functioning through our consciousness by means of the parables thus forms a new environment, canceling the fragmented view of things created by the unaided human intellect.

Chapter 1

The Hidden Treasure

The kingdom of heaven is like treasure hidden in a field, which a man found and covered up; then in his joy he goes and sells all that he has and buys that field.
—Matthew 13:44

Jesus said, "The kingdom is like a man who had a hidden treasure in his field without knowing it. And after he died, he left it to his son. The son did not know about the treasure. He inherited the field and sold it. And the one who bought it went plowing and found the treasure. He began to lend money at interest to whomever he wished."
—Thomas 109

In his book, *Finding Is the First Act: Trove Folktales and Jesus' Treasure Parable*, Crossan reveals how widespread treasure tales are in world literature. We are thus alerted to the great importance of the hidden treasure motif as pointing to a reality within ourselves.

The gospel of Thomas, rediscovered in Egypt in 1945, is a significant source for the parables of Jesus along with Matthew, Mark, and Luke in the New Testament. Whether the gospel of John also contains parables depends on how one defines a parable. John contains many similes as in the other gospels, but those similes are not narratives. On this basis, we are excluding most material from John in this book. This does not mean, however, that the gospel of John is of lesser value as a source for Jesus' teachings, and *no such inference is intended.*

The treasure parables in Matthew and Thomas share the motif of finding a hidden treasure, but they are quite different in detail. Scholars can sometimes reconstruct an original parable by comparing two or more versions.

On the other hand, we must consider that Jesus would have given somewhat similar but not identical parables at different times. So two (or more) forms can be equally authentic, as is the case here.

In the Near East, landowners often buried gold, silver, and other valuable things in the ground, as protection against thieves. They still do this in some areas. If the owner dies, and another person later finds the treasure, he has a legal right to keep it. But rather than getting lost in the niceties of legal claims, let us examine the deeper meaning of the hidden treasure parables.

What a magnificent revelation it is to our thoughts to understand the hidden treasure not as gold coins or jewels, but as the divine presence within our deepest being. The very God who is all-in-all, the divine Creator and Sustainer, is within my body, mind, soul and Spirit. Those who practice quiet, sustained meditation know this to be true. In contemplating the archetypal image of the hidden treasure, we know this gleam of truth as though seeing reflected rays of sunlight flashing from a golden bowl.

How do we build on this flash of insight, how do we make it central to our thoughts on awakening? How do we use this wisdom through the many challenges of a difficult day? How do we use such parables to guide us through dreams at night? We do not need to go into some deserted place and spend hours of sweaty digging with a shovel; all we need to do is in earnest prayer, deepest contemplation, claim our treasure, *realize our true identity which is one with God.* With this claim, the sudden finding of our treasure within, our lives begin to glow with a sense of fulfillment, a sense of having recognized our true destiny. Those about us will perceive a new inner harmony, a health of spirit which will lift our physical well-being, and raise the level of all our accomplishments through the day.

Among the alchemists, as well as others, the treasure motif referred to the highest level of our being. The great treasure is within, not outside ourselves. Carl G. Jung noted that the hidden treasure, the pearl, and the mustard seed all point symbolically to the indwelling Christ.[1] These images point to the integration of the Christ mind into the human soul, resulting in the individual's positive growth and development.

The Gospel of Truth, a second century Valentinian work, refers twice to the hidden treasure. The Logos or indwelling Christ is extolled as a treasure to the seeker, a true path to the lost, illumination to the ignorant, stability to the spiritually drunken, and purity to the defiled.

It is significant that in Matthew 13:44–45, we find the parable of the treasure hidden in the field immediately followed by the merchant finding one pearl of great value. Writing on these life-transforming themes, Crossan notes the importance of their three main verbs which are *finds, buys and sells.* He summarizes the following three steps:

Advent—Discovers the treasure, "which opens up a new world and unforeseen possibilities."

Reversal—Gives up past beliefs and limitations, selling "all that he has."

Action—Obtains the treasure, making available "a new world of life and action."[2]

The great treasure, the indwelling Christ, is "hidden" within our own being. As Elizabeth Boyden Howes declares, commenting on the treasure and the pearl, "the Kingdom is here, present, to be actualized in and by individuals."[3] So it need not remain hidden, if we shift our attention to it. When the man in the parable *finds* the treasure, he willingly *sells* all that he has. This represents a willingness to give up all contrary beliefs and opinions. He then *buys* the treasure. This means to receive, and thus release, this inner reality to heal, harmonize, and inspire us.

The parable emphasizes that the man made the exchange *in his joy.* It is joyful to let go of self-imposed limitations (though this can also be temporarily frightening). It is a joy to claim our heritage as children of God. When a person overcomes some limitation on a subconscious level, energy which had formerly been blocked-off is released. This results in a feeling of joy, peace, and vitality welling up from within.

Advent–reversal–action is thus a theme of great practical importance. The process occurs over and over again, as negative programming is canceled and creative potential is made active.

The version in Thomas adds an element not found in Matthew, a lament over a son who, though he had inherited the field with its treasure, never was aware of the fortune he possessed. How important it is to learn to bring to our conscious awareness the power and joy of the Christ within! Thomas also adds to the story that the new buyer could now lend money at interest to whomever he wished, thus illustrating the ongoing strength of the knowledge of the Christ within.

Affirmations

I am open and receptive to the inner treasure, the Christ.

I am willing to give up the limiting, demeaning thoughts and beliefs of the past.

I am a child of God, with the unlimited nature and potential of infinite Mind. I realize that this is also the truth of every man, woman, and child.

God's ideas are an infinite treasure, which meet every human need.

Chapter 2

The Pearl

⁴⁵**Again, the kingdom of heaven is like a merchant in search of fine pearls, ⁴⁶who, on finding one pearl of great value, went and sold all that he had and bought it.**
—Matthew 13:45-46

Jesus said, "The kingdom of the father is like a merchant who had a consignment of merchandise and who discovered a pearl. That merchant was shrewd. He sold the merchandise and bought the pearl alone for himself."
—Thomas 76

Jesus spoke all, or at a minimum nearly all, of his parables in the Aramaic language. In so doing, he began many of the parables with the datival introduction. In this original tongue, where the English translation reads, "the kingdom of heaven is like a merchant in search of fine pearls..." he actually said the equivalent of, "*It is the case with* the kingdom of heaven *as with* a merchant in search of fine pearls...." The point is that the parable does not equate the kingdom with the merchant himself, but with *the end result or conclusion of the narrative.* In other words, the kingdom is identified with the result of the merchant finding–selling–*buying the pearl,* especially the last of the list, through which the full dominion and enjoyment of the kingdom comes.

The merchant is the actor—thus *the element of choice within the individual.* The pearl is the Christ, which is our true spiritual identity, one with God. The Christ is God's eternal idea of us, the basic reality that unites us with the one Mind and thus with everyone and with all the universe.

The gospel of Matthew usually prefers the term, "kingdom

of heaven"; the gospel of Thomas, "kingdom of the Father."
The gospels of Mark and Luke prefer "kingdom of God." These
distinctions are merely literary, and may be more the work of
the compilers than of Jesus himself.

Jesus, in his teaching, linked the images of the treasure and
the pearl. The parables listed in Matthew 13 are scattered
throughout the gospel of Thomas, which convincingly shows
they were *not* all given on the same occasion. Nevertheless, the
linkage between the treasure in Matthew 13:44 and the pearl in
13:45–46 is probably original. For the parable of the pearl in
Thomas 76 is followed by the statement, "You, too, seek his
unfailing and enduring *treasure* where no moth comes near to
devour and no worm destroys." This resembles Matthew 6:20.

In the ancient world, people placed great value on pearls.
Pearl divers worked in the Red Sea and other ocean areas. The
wealthier classes sought them, and wore them in necklaces. The
common people tended to venerate them to the point of super-
stition. A folk belief existed that whoever owned a pearl would
always be happy.

The magnitude of the energy of the pearl as a symbol of
something greater can hardly be overestimated. Its beauty as a
jewel, and its great monetary value, were stepping stones on the
way for the common people to imagine its far greater worth as
a token for ultimate reach into the spiritual. As a jewel with its
soft luminescent hues, it is a symbol of the love nature of
Christ. In the simplicity of its glowing beauty it is saying, "Yes,
God is here." From the bed of the ocean floor—taken from the
body of one of the simplest, yet marvelous creatures, the oyster—comes this acknowledgement of the omnipresence of God.

With our hand on the soft pearl, feeling it on a ring, or
lying in a necklace against our chest, may we be reminded that
even as this pearl was found in an oyster, so too can we draw
from the one, invisible, infinite source of supply for everything
we need. This touch of God's presence in created beauty in the
outer world can open our souls to the reality of the overshadow-
ing beauty of the spiritual; it is one of the most valuable
insights we can have. This experience, this link between rare
beauty in the physical, and vision of the beyond, should assist

us in knowing ourselves as more than skin and bones, more than brains and blood; we will learn to know ourselves in deepest reality as eternal souls.

To claim this truth for our own, however, we have to let go of all sorts of limiting beliefs about ourselves and our capacities. We are not to view our essential being from the standpoint of sin and guilt. Rather, our foremost appraisal should be seeing ourselves as heirs to the kingdom of God, one with God's love, joy, and peace.

The pearl is also an archetypal symbol of wisdom. Job 28:18 suggests this by stating, "The price of wisdom is above pearls." A third century work, the gospel of Philip, is more explicit. It contains another interesting parable of the pearl:

> When the pearl is cast down into the mud it does not become greatly despised, nor if it is anointed with balsam oil will it become more precious. But it always has value in the eyes of its owner. Compare the sons of God, wherever they may be. They still have value in the eyes of their Father.[4]

Returning to Jesus' parable in Matthew and Thomas, we find that *a merchant* pursues the pearl. This points to the practical side of the issue, which is explicit in Thomas: "That merchant was shrewd. He sold the merchandise and bought the pearl alone for himself." Here again the genius of Jesus shines clearly. He lifts us above mundane concerns, and at the same time keeps us from a life-rejecting negativism. The pearl is not only the greatest spiritual truth; when we learn to apply it mentally, it is also the most practical. In so doing, we bring forth health, wisdom, love, and abundance from the all-sufficient ideas of the mind of God.

Here the question of value is of key importance. A wise merchant can tell the difference between superior and inferior goods, and between the real and the counterfeit. What applies in the market-place is equally important to the affairs of the soul. We need to tell the difference between superior and inferior ways of thinking, and even between true and false belief systems.

In the parable, the merchant buys the highest quality goods at a relatively cheap price. This brings profit, and it only appears to be loss to one who does not know the market. By the same token, to give up or "sell" the negative, the illusion of separation from God, is only sacrifice from a superficial point of view. It is profit from the standpoint of what is gained: conscious companionship with our divine Father-Mother, and all-sufficiency in all things.

Clement and Origen of Alexandria both quoted Jesus as saying: "Be approved money-changers." This is not in the Bible, but it is probably an authentic oral tradition. The Sadducees in Jerusalem accepted coins and gave temple money in exchange—for a cut. They skillfully looked at and handled these coins, and dropped them to catch their precise sound. They could readily tell the difference between the real and the counterfeit. Our work as "approved money-changers" is to examine our own thoughts, feelings, and beliefs, and to weigh them according to the standard of the pearl of great price.

Affirmations

I am open and receptive to the pearl of great price, the Indwelling Christ.

At the core of my being, I AM the Christ. As an individual expression of God, I have the mind of Christ.

I am not an heir to sin, disease, or death. I am a son and heir of God, and a joint-heir with Jesus the Christ.

I realize and enjoy conscious oneness with all that God is.

I learn to apply this truth in practical ways, in mind, body, and affairs.

Chapter 3

The Great Fish

And he said, "The man is like a wise fisherman who cast his net into the sea and drew it up from the sea full of small fish. Among them the wise fisherman found a fine large fish. He threw all the small fish back into the sea and chose the large fish without difficulty. Whoever has ears to hear, let him hear."

—Thomas 8

This parable, lost for 1,500 years, was rediscovered as part of the gospel of Thomas in 1945. Its images resemble those of the parable of the fish net (Matthew 13:47–48). Nevertheless, the great fish is an independent parable. Its meaning is similar to the hidden treasure and the pearl, sharing the basic structure of advent–reversal–action.

The archetypal nature of the fish image is reflected in mythological uses. For example, in the *Anabasis*, the Greek general Xenophon (approx. 434–355 B.C.) mentions sacred fish in the Chalus River, venerated by the local people. In a later period, Lucian (second century A.D.) wrote a book called *The Syrian Goddess*. This Greek rationalist satirizes the Syrian practice of venerating fish. In the cult of Atargatis, the members ate fish as a kind of ritual communion. The Syrian Christians, knowing of these practices, may have found Jesus' fish parables to be of special interest. Note that only the gospel of Matthew, probably compiled in Syrian Antioch, preserves the parable of the fish net.

The validity of the fish symbol is well documented. This is true from both the historical and the archetypal points of view.[5] In this connection, a general statement should be made regarding Bible interpretation:

19

Historical evidence, in the more restrictive sense, is logically limited by a time frame. That is to say, for one literary or cultural factor to influence another, both must meet in the same space at the same time. It must, moreover, be something that can be physically seen, heard, or touched.

Archetypal evidence, to the contrary, need not have occurred in a certain space or sequence to be relevant. Collective images persist for thousands of years, and can be contacted anywhere on the planet earth. In addition, part of the evidence is subjective, in the form of dreams, visions, and images seen in meditation.

Returning to our text, the fisherman threw his net into the sea, expecting a routine catch. Instead, he found an enormous fish along with the rest. The small ones, of little account, he threw back and kept the prized fish. A real-life fisherman would probably do the same.

Each of the figures has a symbolic meaning. The *fisherman with his net* represents the conscious mind. The *sea with its fish* is the subconscious mind and its abundant contents, both personal and collective. The *great fish,* however, is the indwelling Christ.

A few comments will suffice to show the relevance of the great fish symbol. From the standpoint of astrology, Jesus appeared at the start of the age of Pisces, the Fish. Christians used the simple outline of a fish as their identifying symbol, a sign of their presence to other followers of the way, as they were first called. The simple design of a fish is featured in the earliest gatherings of Christians in the catacombs of Rome. Tertullian, in apparent reference to the parable, wrote (about 200 A.D.): "We are little fishes in Christ our great fish." In fact, the Greek word for fish, *ichthus,* became a cryptogram for the Christ:

Greek Letter	Eng. Equiv.	Greek Word	English Trans.
iota	I	'Iησους	Jesus
chi	CH	Χριστός	Christ
theta	TH	θεóυ	of God
upsilon	U	Υιós	(the) Son
sigma	S	Σωτήρ	Savior or Healer

Other data point to *eating the fish*, which the parable does not specifically mention. For example, the early Christians ate fish at the *love feast*, which was the original communion service. To Augustine of Hippo, Christ was the eucharistically eaten fish. Also, Tobit 6:1-5, in the Apocrypha, tells the story of a "healing fish," of which Tobias eats its gall, heart, and liver. Jesus develops the themes of advent–reversal–action as follows:

(1) *Advent*—The wise fisherman, to his complete surprise, finds this huge fish in his net. From one point of view, we lift the Christ mind out of unconsciousness into our conscious awareness. This is illusory, however, because the Christ mind is always fully conscious and the process works in the reverse direction. That is to say, the Christ in us awakens our personal mind from a preoccupation with outer appearances—a kind of sleep—and revitalizes it with a vivid sense of the divine presence. We do not need to awaken the Christ mind, but awaken to its indwelling presence and power.

(2) *Reversal*—We have to make a choice as to what we will allow to occupy our consciousness. We cannot abide in the mind of Christ, and also cling to every sort of "trash fish." Only with constant focus on divine ideas is real progress possible. The symbolism is simple, unforgettable; the wise choice is to land the great fish, the indwelling Christ, and to reject contrary thoughts and beliefs.

(3) *Action*—The final implicit step, after landing the great fish, is to cook and eat it. This means to *assimilate* the Christ mind and its perfect ideas into our everyday lives. It is to incorporate the expression of wholeness and harmony through our thoughts, emotions, words, actions, body, relationships, and conditions. This is not something that is unnatural or inherently difficult. It is the natural unfoldment of our true eternal nature as children of God.

Our parable ends, "Whoever has ears to hear, let him hear."[6] We often find that Jesus' parables have closing statements that became attached to them at a later date. This may or may not apply to the ending here. In any case, it is entirely appropriate as a call to be open and receptive to the great fish, the indwelling Christ.

In summary, Jesus sought to reveal a timeless reality which we can demonstrate here and now. We can receive the Christ mind into awareness, reject any distractions to its rule within us, and assimilate its qualities of love, life, truth, joy, and peace. The salvation/healing that Jesus offers is an ongoing process, in which we bring more and more of our real, God-given nature and potential into expression. As stated in a biblical paradox, we are God's children now, but it does not yet fully appear what we will be.

Affirmations

I am awakened into the consciousness of the great fish, the Christ.

I let go of all contrary images and beliefs.

I let the transforming power of God's love have its full way in me. I am the expression of love in my thoughts, feelings, words, and actions.

I let the transforming power of God's life have its full way in me. I am healed and whole in soul and body.

I let the transforming power of God's truth have its full way in me. I think true ideas. I am rightly guided in all my ways.

I enjoy the present moment, with the knowledge that the divine Spirit is completing its perfect work in me.

Chapter 4

The Cloth and Wineskins

[21]"No one sews a piece of unshrunk cloth on an old garment; if he does, the patch tears away from it, the new from the old, and a worse tear is made. [22]And no one puts new wine into old wineskins; if he does, the wine will burst the skins, and the wine is lost, and so are the skins; but new wine is for fresh skins."
    —*Mark 2:21-22 (parallel passages: Matthew 9:16-17;*
    Luke 5:36-39; Thomas 47)

Some parables became paired together in later tradition. In the case of the cloth and wineskins, however, it is certain that Jesus presented them as twin parables. All four sources link them together, and their meanings are similar.

The four versions differ somewhat. The gospel of Thomas, for example, mentions the old and new cloth in the reverse order, stating: "An *old* patch is not sewn onto a *new* garment, because a tear would result." Both Luke and Thomas mention that no one first drinks the old wine, and then desires the new. Also, Thomas includes a couplet, a literary form familiar to the ancient Jews:

> New wine is not put into old wineskins,
>   lest they burst;
> nor is old wine put into a new wineskin,
>   lest it spoil it.

Jesus probably spoke these twin parables more than once, in a somewhat different form. All versions make a point of contrasting the "old" and the "new." Their interpretation rests on how we define this contrast. The first three gospels (the synoptic—as seen with one eye) link these parables to a statement about fasting, and a wedding feast (Matthew 9:14-15; Mark 2:18-20; Luke 5:33-35). The gospel of Thomas does not do so, but lists a somewhat similar passage separately in Saying 104.

Luke 5:33-35, following the synoptic context, reads:

> And they said to him, "The disciples of John fast often and offer prayers, and so do the disciples of the Pharisees, but yours eat and drink." And Jesus said to them, "Can you make wedding guests fast while the bridegroom is with them? The days will come, when the bridegroom is taken away from them, and then they will fast in those days."

The evidence, then, suggests that Jesus sometimes—but not always—gave these two parables with reference to old and new religious practices. In our example, John the Baptist's followers fasted but Jesus' disciples did not. Their version in Thomas, however, cautions us not to limit their meaning to a religious or ceremonial framework only. Even when applied to a specific situation, they point in principle to the need for a radical change in consciousness, as we shall shortly see.

Let us briefly review the cultural background. Many of the common people were so poor that they owned only one robe. They would continue to patch it until it was too worn to use. Only then would they buy a new one. If they used a new and unshrunk piece of cloth as a patch, it would be heavier and soon would pull away from the old garment. Beholding the tear larger than before, their hearts would be dismayed with these fruitless efforts at protecting themselves against blowing sand, too hot rays of the sun, and cold nights.

Contrary to the King James translation, people didn't keep unfermented wine in bottles. If they had done so, the corks would have popped off when it fermented. Rather, they kept wine in goatskins. They cut off the goat's head, and took out the insides. Then they tied the hide shut at the legs and neck. A small opening was left at the neck to let the gas escape from the fermenting wine.

New wineskins are soft and pliable, but the old skins are hard and rigid. New wine can be poured safely into the new skins, but the old skins would burst from the fermentation. The wine would then be lost, and the containers rendered useless.

The old and new garments represent opposite belief systems. This is implicit in Leviticus 19:19 which declares: "You shall not sow your field with two kinds of seed; nor shall there come upon you *a garment of cloth made of two kinds of stuff.*" The "old" garment is a view in which things are fragmented and devoid of the active life and power of God. The "new" garment is the vision of the universe in its omnipresent oneness, whole and complete in God. It means a transformed consciousness, which—when enough people share this vision—holds the promise of a new era of spiritual enlightenment.

Ervin Seale sums up the issue succinctly when he writes: "God says that he made a good world and he approves of it [cf. Genesis 1:31]. But man is inclined to disagree, and his disagreement costs him his peace and pleasure in this world."[7] And, in the parable, Jesus is saying in effect: It is useless to try to patch up one's old ways of thinking and living with a few new thoughts, while holding onto the rest. It is better to throw away the old, rotten garment, and to put on the new one.

Too often our current pattern of life has been a complaining about this and that, doing little to help ourselves or to serve others. The parable of the cloth likens that life-style to a worn-out coat, which must someday be cast aside. Then we are to find and put on new garments, new ways of living suitable to the being of light, the Christ-light, which is at our central core.

Jesus' intent becomes clearer when we review other examples of the old/new garment motif. The book of Isaiah, which Jesus sometimes quoted, has several passages that relate to this theme: 14:24–27; 25:6–9; 34:4; 54:10; 64:6. Psalm 102:26–28 is also significant. Isaiah 25:6–8 links the images of *feasting, wine, a veil,* and *the veil's removal:*

> On this mountain the Lord of Hosts will prepare
> a banquet of rich fare for all the peoples,
> a banquet of wines well matured and richest fare,
> well-matured wines strained clear.
> On this mountain the Lord will swallow up
> that veil that shrouds all the peoples,

the pall thrown over all the nations;
he will swallow up death for ever.
Then the Lord God will wipe away the tears from every
    face
and remove the reproach of his people from the whole
    earth.
The Lord has spoken.
(New English Bible)

An extracanonical work, *The Odes of Solomon,* declares
    (11:10–12):
And I rejected the folly cast upon the earth,
And stripped it off and cast it from me.
And the Lord renewed me with His garment,
And possessed me by His light.
And from above He gave me immortal rest,
And I became like the land that blossoms and rejoices in its
    fruits.[8]

The parable of the wineskins makes a related point. We
cannot expect to contain the new wine of spiritual consciousness within old beliefs and customs that are no longer useful.
This would match the folly of pouring new wine into old, rigid
wineskins. The fermentation would destroy the skins, and the
new wine would be lost. The Holy Spirit's inspiring, quickening
power needs to be poured into "fresh skins," i.e. into a new and
more positive way of thinking and doing things.

Wine, in the Bible, is a symbol of divine inspiration. This
meaning is apparent in accounts of the last supper, but is not
limited to these scenes. For example, in the book of Job, Elihu
declares:

For I am full of words,
the spirit within me constrains me.
Behold, my heart is like wine that has no vent;
like new wineskins, it is ready to burst.

                                        —Job 32:18–19

Wine also became a symbol of the new era of enlightenment. In the book of Revelation, an angel declares: "Put in your

sickle, and gather the clusters of the vine of the earth, for its grapes are ripe" (Revelation 14:18).

Finally, in the allegory of the vine, Jesus declared: "I am the vine, you are the branches. He who abides in me, and I in him, he it is that bears much fruit, for apart from me you can do nothing" (John 15:5). When the implications of this allegory are fully accepted, it shatters the old belief system based on duality, evil, and separation. We awaken to find ourselves inseparably linked, with Jesus and with all others, in the cosmic Christ. Our dominant interest is then to abide in the mind of Christ, on the basis of which we bear fruit in the free, abundant, joyful life for which we have been created.

Affirmations

I throw off the old garment of error, duality, and limitation.

I am clothed with the new garment of truth, oneness, and liberty.

I accept the new wine of the Spirit. I am illumined, inspired, and made whole.

Section II–
SOWING AND REAPING

While the earth remains, seedtime and harvest, cold and heat, summer and winter, day and night, shall not cease.
–Genesis 8:22

To reach his listeners, Jesus used familiar images from daily life. His seed parables reflect archetypes which developed with the beginning of agriculture many thousands of years ago. He likened natural reproduction—whether human, animal, or plant—to the law of creative consciousness. The fundamental point is that *like produces like*. This applies to thoughts and feelings as certainly as it does to wheat, oats, and rye.

The parables discussed in Chapters 1–4 reveal the mind-transforming nature of the kingdom of God. With the coming of higher understanding, a person makes a clear-cut break with past ways of thinking and doing things. Again we see that this involves the three steps of *advent, reversal,* and *action*.

However, the seed parables have a different emphasis. They center in the third step, *action*. Spiritual laws are to be applied in specific ways. The initial realization of our Christ nature is followed by a process of activating, using, and assimilating its qualities.

Our new vision of oneness does not leave us in a vacuum. A new pattern of continuity, of mental and spiritual law, energizes our thought processes. This pattern is more dependable than the unstable material beliefs that it replaces. Central to it is the law of cause and effect, of sowing and reaping, of action and reaction. Jesus compares this to another triad, *planting, growth,* and *harvest*. The parables of the seed growing secretly, and the wheat and the tares, apply this theme with special clarity.

29

Many of us, from experience over the years, feel we are unable to change for the better. We know that there is a vast gulf between our life-style and the way of Christ. Nevertheless, we have found that breaking old habits, comfortable ways, is beyond us. The dieter, who lost fifty pounds, a year later finds himself or herself weighing more than ever. While the diet was successful, entering into a continuing life-style was not. If we have made valiant efforts to move into a more worthy, deeper spiritual life, and failed again and again, the parables of the seed can sustain us with a never-dying hope.

A seed is an organized potential, with the ability to fulfill itself. An acorn seems dead on its surface, but in it lies the potential to become a great and majestic oak tree. Between the seed and the finished tree is a miraculous process of growth. The very commonness of this activity in nature leads us to forget its remarkable character.

An idea is also an organized potential. The seed parables deal with this fact from both an absolute and a relative point of view. In *The Parable of the Sower*, the Christ mind ever sows true ideas in the individual soul. Indeed, our Christ identity is already the perfect effect of a perfect cause. In practical terms, this means that each of us has an unlimited capacity for mental and spiritual growth and awakening. In *The Seed Growing Secretly*, the individual sows by thinking. Through the law of cause and effect, of planting thoughts in a subjective ground, we finally reap what we have sown.

Walter Wink, in his insightful book *The Bible in Human Transformation*, declares: "He who would master the world without relation to its ground and origin thus plays the Devil."[1] This expresses the folly of believing that just pushing harder with our mind and hands on the levers of the external world will bring us to spiritual maturity. Faster cars, more splendid homes, and huge bank accounts do not guarantee true happiness. On the other hand, spiritual energies released into the outer world can have continuing success. The seed parables show how tiny seeds of divine power, released through prayer, or through simple acts of caring, can bring lasting stability in our seeking for life's greatest goals.

Jesus apparently gave more seed parables than are found in the Bible. The Apocryphon of James, found at Nag Hammadi and compiled in the second century A.D., probably includes some authentic sayings of Jesus. It preserves three parables: the palm shoot, the grain of wheat, and the ear of grain (#28, #29, and #30 in Crossan's Workbook). The last two are congruent with Jesus' seed parables that are available elsewhere.

Chapter 5

The Sower (#1)

²**And he taught them many things in parables, and in his teaching he said to them:** ³**"Listen! A sower went out to sow.** ⁴**And as he sowed, some seed fell along [the original Aramaic can be translated "*on*"] the path, and the birds came and devoured it.** ⁵**Other seed fell on rocky ground, where it had not much soil, and immediately it sprang up, [since it had no depth of soil;** ⁶**and when the sun rose it was scorched,] and since it had no root it withered away.** ⁷**Other seed fell among thorns and the thorns grew up and choked it, and it yielded no grain.** ⁸**And other seeds fell into good soil and brought forth grain, growing up and increasing and yielding thirtyfold and sixtyfold and a hundredfold."** ⁹**And he said, "He who has ears to hear, let him hear."**

–Mark 4:2–9 (parallel passages: Matthew 13:3–9;
Luke 8:4–8; Thomas 9)

The sower is not only a parable, but a key to all the parables. Mark 4:13 reads: "And he [Jesus] said to them, 'Do you not understand this parable? How then will you understand all the parables?' " *The key is the basic polarity that exists between two levels of consciousness.* These are *the Christ mind,* which is universal and unconditioned, and *the conscious phase of mind,* which is individual and local. The One is in the many, and the many are in the One. The Christ in a cosmic sense is our basic, eternal Identity. On a personal level, various reactions to the Christ are possible. Specifically, the four conditions of soil in the parable of the sower represent four types of human response. All the parables, however, relate to this polarity in one way or another. It is their unifying theme.

One of the questions confronting readers of the words of Jesus is, "Am I really understanding the meaning of the parables, or am I just skimming the surface?" His words as given in Mark 4:11–12 haunt us:

> And he said to them, "To you has been given the secret of the kingdom of God, but for those outside everything is in parables; so that they may indeed see but not perceive, and may indeed hear but not understand; lest they should turn again, and be forgiven."

With these words paraphrased from Isaiah 6:9–10, Jesus tells us that there is a surface level of the parables open to all, but their deeper meaning is only open to those who understand the "secret of the kingdom of God." It is part of the paradox of Jesus' teaching that the same parables served to *conceal* the nature of the kingdom from some hearers, and to *reveal* it to others. We have already indicated what this "secret" may be. Our outward, daily consciousness is superimposed upon a deeper Christ consciousness. We know this must be so, because we are all the living expression of God. As Wordsworth stated, we came into the world "trailing clouds of glory," but settled into a life-style not unlike a hard shell, failing to acknowledge our true, deep nature. When we look past this "hard shell" of habit and conditioned responses, the "secret" of the parables begins to become clear. In this light, the "seed" parables begin to glow with new meaning.

It is important to note that these mystifying words, "that they may see, but not perceive...lest they should turn again," have been clarified by the eminent parables scholar, Joachim Jeremias. Saying that Jesus would not wilfully keep anyone in ignorance, he points out that in the original Aramaic, verse 12 would end: "*unless* they turn and are forgiven."

As already stated, the same parables served to *conceal* the nature of the kingdom from some hearers, and to *reveal* it to others. In a larger sense, everything we experience in life is colored by the way that we perceive it. Thus, if his listeners were closed in mind and heart, the parables would either mean nothing, or else become a mirror to reflect their own prejudices back to them. On the other hand, if they had "ears to hear," i.e. were inwardly open and receptive, *and put all dogmas and pre-conceptions aside,* the parables became a mighty vehicle to reveal the inner kingdom to them. This is still true for readers today.

In many cases, our sources differ *as to who* the audience was for a given parable. We can distinguish three classes: (1) Jesus' disciples, (2) his adversaries, and (3) the crowds. For example, according to the gospels of Matthew and Thomas, Jesus spoke the parable of the leaven to his disciples. The gospel of Luke has him deliver this parable to the general public.

With their dual potential to either conceal or reveal truth, however, depending on the attitude of *each individual hearer,* recovering a given parable's original context(s) is not essential. If it were, our hopes of understanding many of them would be greatly diminished; our data as to context is limited and often misleading. Happily, though, we do not have to establish a *sitz im leben,* life situation, for every parable, as some German scholars insist we do. The parables' universal meanings can function well, apart from temporary or local situations. This is the strength of ages-old archetypes; their essential structure can be understood in France or Italy, the Orient or Latin America.

As Norman Perrin wrote, "The historical factors should be taken into account insofar as, but *only* insofar as, this is demanded by the text itself."[2]

All three biblical versions of *the sower* are followed by interpretative commentary: Matthew 13:18-23, Mark 4:14-20, and Luke 8:11-15. These interpretations are probably not original with Jesus; more likely they were added in transmission by later scribes. They are not fully consistent among themselves. The author of Thomas entirely omits these commentaries, indicating that this material was not in his sources. This is not to deny the value of some of the points made in these sections. It is beyond the scope of this book, however, to comment upon them in detail.

In addition, we need to question the section: "since it had no depth of soil; and when the sun rose it was scorched." Luke and Thomas both omit this reading. Also, it does not accord with nature to claim that the seed sprang up *because* the soil lacked depth. Thinness of soil does not stimulate a plant's growth, but severely limits it. On the other hand, it makes good sense to narrate: "Other seed fell on rocky ground, where it had not much soil, and immediately it sprang up...and since it had no root it withered away." It is safe to infer, from the contents of Jesus' parables, that he was in close rapport with the earth and its processes. Therefore, he would not have been imprecise in speaking of such things.

A later editor added the section on the hot sun. He did so with good motive, to encourage his fellow Christians during a time of persecution. The scorching sun is a fit metaphor for the trials that they faced.

Mark 4:16–17 proves that some elements of the early church applied the passage in question to persecution:

> And these in like manner are the ones sown upon rocky ground, who, when they hear the word, immediately receive it with joy; and they have no root in themselves, but endure for a while; then, when tribulation or persecution arises on account of the word, immediately they fall away.

Considered in its original forms(s), the parable of the sower correctly depicts farming conditions in ancient Galilee. A farmer didn't plant wheat in straight rows, as modern farmers do in the western world. A man would take a sackful of seed grain, and as he walked along would scatter it on the land, one handful at a time. Only after so doing would he plow his field.

He followed these practices with uneven results. Some seeds might fall on a path, or where he had walked and trampled the ground. The birds might eat them before he could do the plowing. Other seeds fell on rocky ground, which is common in that part of the world. Still other seeds fell among thorns. Still others landed on good soil, fertile and without rocks or weeds.

A sower, and the planting of seeds, represented a teacher sowing ideas and information. This referred not only to a human teacher-student relationship, but also to a sowing of truth from the Spirit within. In Jeremiah 31:33, we read: "I will

put my law within them, and I will write it upon their hearts."
And, in the Apocrypha, II Esdras (approx. 90 A.D.) declares:

> For behold, I sow my law in you, and it shall bring forth
> fruit in you, and you shall be glorified through it for ever.
> But though our fathers received the law, they did not keep
> it, and did not observe the statutes; yet the fruit of the law
> did not perish—for it could not, because it was thine. Yet
> those who received it perished, because they did not keep
> what had been sown in them.
>
> —II Esdras 9:31–33

In the first epistle of John, seed represents divine ideas.
The avoidance of sin is a by-product of keeping in contact with
God's ideas:

> A child of God does not commit sin, because the divine
> seed remains in him; he cannot be a sinner, because he is
> God's child.
>
> —1 John 3:9 (New English Bible)

It is evident that the sower in Jesus' parable—as is the case
with the treasure, pearl, and great fish—represents the
indwelling Christ. It is our basic identity, ever one with God.
This sower broadcasts divine ideas to the soul, everywhere and
at all times. Through this story, Jesus wanted to emphasize *the
constant nature of the Christ mind and its action,* not just the fulfillment of a process.

Mark's powerful style begins and ends with calls to *be open*
and *be receptive* to the sower. The Greek wording is here almost
certainly based on the Hebrew word *shema,* which appears frequently in the Old Testament. It means *hear and obey,* as in
Deuteronomy 6:4: "Hear O Israel, the Lord our God is one
Lord."

> And he taught them many things in parables, and in his
> teaching he said to them: "Listen! A sower went out to
> sow" (4:2–3).
> And he said, "He who has ears to hear, let him hear"(4:9).

The sower goes forth to sow, and the seeds fall on four types of ground: (1) on a path, (2) on rocky ground, (3) on an area where thorns are growing, and (4) on good and productive soil. Different soils, or course, respond differently to the same type and quality of seed. In the same way, various people respond differently to the same spiritual ideas and teachings. Each type of ground represents a different attitude that one can take toward the Christ mind. We can be any kind of hearer that we choose to be.

> *And as he sowed, some seed fell along* (Aramaic—on) *the path, and the birds came and devoured it* (4:4).

The hard, compacted soil is a symbol of a closed mind. Dogmatists and negative thinkers of all types prevent the seed of divine ideas from sprouting in their souls, and thus in their everyday lives. As Paul observed: "The unspiritual man does not receive the gifts of the Spirit of God, for they are folly to him, and he is not able to understand them because they are spiritually discerned" (1 Corinthians 2:14).

Since the sower is active everywhere and at all times, however, the path to progress is ever open. At any time we sincerely and wholeheartedly seek wisdom, we will receive it. The desire we feel for wisdom is itself the action of the sower within us.

> *Other seed fell on rocky ground, where it had not much soil, and immediately it sprang up...and since it had no root it withered away* (4:5–6).

The most vital stage in the life of a plant is after it has sprouted, but before it has grown deep roots. A good gardener knows this. He keeps the ground watered so that the roots can develop. Once this occurs, less attention is needed. On rocky ground, however, roots don't grow properly and the plant will wither and die.

Divine ideas also need to be nurtured with care. They need to be firmly established *on a subconscious level,* and grow deeper and deeper roots there. Otherwise, spiritual progress will be temporary and initial gains lost.

In the parable, the plant withered "since it had no root." This implies that we need a clear realization of the root, or spiritual source, of our being. An acceptance in theory is not enough. Regular meditation on divine reality, the practice of the presence of God, makes the difference.

> *Other seed fell among thorns and the thorns grew up and choked it, and it yielded no grain* (4:7).

A diligent farmer or gardener weeds his land often. Thorns not only crowd out other plants; they also sap the soil of vital nutrients. (If you have seen a field of grain with large thistles in it, you know what I mean.) The third type of hearer, then, is one who has certain Christ ideas rooted in his or her soul, but lets other interests crowd them out.

Action is necessary in two respects. First, we pull out the thorns of negative beliefs and attitudes from our soul. Also, we weed out frivolous interests, so that we have the time and energy to think and do the things that are for our highest good. By taking these steps, we give the positive ideas and resources of the kingdom a chance to grow and increase within us. The use of affirmations, positive mental picturing, and daily meditation make the difference between a mental weed patch and a garden in which the fruits of the Spirit thrive.

> *And other seeds fell into good soil and brought forth grain, growing up and increasing and yielding thirtyfold and sixtyfold and a hundredfold* (4:8).

The good soil symbolizes the fourth kind of hearer. Those of us who are open and receptive to divine ideas, and think, speak, and live according to their nature, will be tremendously benefited. The yields given here are far above what was normally expected. This is intentional exaggeration, for an actual ear of wheat will not exceed forty grains. Thus, as in Genesis 26:12, the natural growth process is increased to a miracle yield: "And Isaac sowed in that land, and reaped in the same year a hundredfold." This implies that the yields available through divine

grace are far greater than those yielded through the mental law
of cause and effect.

The words translated *brought forth* and *yielding* actually
mean "kept on bringing forth," and "continuing to yield."
Charles Torrey confirms that the original Aramaic, on which
the Greek is based, means "yielded fruit IN CONSTANT
INCREASE."[3] The parable, then, does not refer to a one-shot
deal. It teaches a continuing unfoldment of good into everyday
experience, even to a thirty-, sixty-, and hundredfold increase.

Affirmations

I am open and receptive to the sower, the indwelling
Christ. I have the mind of Christ.

I set aside all preconceptions. I am taught by the perfect
inner teacher, who knows all things.

In returning and rest I am made whole. In quietness and
confidence is my strength.

I am kept in perfect peace. My soul is centered in the one
Mind that is perfect life, perfect love, and perfect peace.

Chapter 6

The Seed Growing Secretly

²⁶**And he said, "The kingdom of God is as if a man should scatter seed upon the ground, ²⁷and should sleep and rise night and day, and the seed should sprout and grow, he knows not how. ²⁸The earth produces of itself, first the blade, then the ear, then the full grain in the ear. ²⁹But when the grain is ripe, at once he puts in the sickle, because the harvest has come."**

—Mark 4:26–29

In verse 29, Jesus cites Joel 3:13: "Put in the sickle, for the harvest is ripe." The prophet Joel expected the day of the Lord, but by that he meant a day of retribution for Near Eastern nations, and the exaltation of Judah. In the parable, by contrast, Jesus rejects the day of the Lord as coming at a particular time. He also implicitly rejects the literal expectation of a final war in heaven and on earth. Instead, he compares the coming of the kingdom of God to planting–growth–harvest, in which "the earth produces of itself"—a basic natural process which is gradual but certain. The coming of the kingdom of God, declares Jesus, is as reaping what has been sown. Wherever good seed has been sown in the mind of the individual, there, in good time, an inner kingdom of the divine grows to completion.

We note that in the previous parable, the sower was the universal Christ, while in this one, the sower is the individual. The sowing is accomplished by the active thought of the conscious phase of mind. As this takes place, however, much more is taking place in our total being. In the apt imagery of the sower, the conscious mind sows thoughts and beliefs into *the ground,* which represents the subconscious phase of mind. The

41

seeds are our thoughts and beliefs. The thoughts we dwell upon become part of our larger personality; implanted in the subconscious, they become established there as patterns of emotion, habit, memory, and action. Producing after their kind, positive thoughts create positive results, and negative thoughts will just as surely breed negative results.

There are close analogies between *visible nature,* and *the mind's creative law.* For example, seeds do not cease to exist when they are plowed under the ground, and out of view. They sprout at a later time. The same is true with thoughts in the mind.

Various frameworks of thought, imagery, and emotion have developed over millennia, in the collective consciousness of humanity. We now surmise that Jesus, in the parables, was dealing with much more than a visible, mechanistic view of reality. Rather, he was pointing to mental energies of cause and effect, not only within an individual life-span, but lasting over many generations. Bad seed or good, whichever is sown in individuals, families, tribes, or nations will produce after its kind.

Seeds need nourishment to grow into mature plants. This includes heat, light, water, and fertilizer. Thoughts respond to nourishment of a different kind—meditation, affirmation, faith, confidence, persistence, and visualization. (This is not to deny that plants also respond to mental pictures and emotions, as demonstrated by Cleve Backster, Frank Loehr, and others.)

"First the blade, then the ear, then the full grain in the ear." The progress of a plant is gradual, with a number of steps on the way to maturity. Likewise, when we are working toward some goal in life, progress is not always immediate. It is usually made by degrees. Even where there has been a revolution of thought, there is an evolutionary process of working out the full expression and implications of the new.

A seed is an organized potential, with the pattern of fulfillment within itself. The same is true of an idea. Any trend of thought that we entertain will produce fruit in our lives. Note that no farmer would randomly plant every type of seed in his field. We also need to be highly selective in what we plant in our own subconscious mind. If we select only positive seeds, the parable is one of great promise. It becomes obvious that we can bring greater good into our lives in any form we desire.

This same parable gives an excellent and concise summary on effective prayer:

(1) *Planting–The kingdom of God is as if a man should scatter seed upon the ground.* A farmer must plant his seeds, or there will be no crop. In the same way, ideas must be planted and ideals mentally pictured, or there will be no result. It is needful to think the thought, to speak the word, to affirm and meditate upon the goal.

(2) *Growth–And should sleep and rise night and day, and the seed should sprout and grow, he knows not how.* A farmer, after planting his seeds, does not strain mentally to make them sprout. Nor, if he knows what he is doing, will he dig them up now and then to see if they are germinating. He knows and accepts with confidence that they will grow. Similarly, in scientific prayer, personal will is to be relaxed, especially when the planting of ideas has been made. Mental strain, worry, and anxiety will delay or prevent the "answer." In prayer as in farming, the power to bring forth the desired results rests with God.

(3) *Harvest–But when the grain is ripe, at once he puts in the sickle, because the harvest has come.* The third step is to accept the results as they appear. Sometimes prayers are "answered" in a way different from what we had expected. A courageous act of will may be necessary. To claim our good, we sometimes have to revise personal relationships, change plans, move to a distant city, or even change basic beliefs. Timing is also important; for while there is no time in Spirit, there is an orderly sequence in which events unfold. This also applies to farming. If a wheat farmer reaped his crop too soon, the moisture content would be too great and the grain would rot in storage. If he waited too long, the crop might be damaged by a storm.

Let us remember that though steps one and three require individual action, step two—of growth or increase—is entirely of the Spirit. As Paul wrote in 1 Corinthians 3:7, "So neither he who plants nor he who waters is anything, but only God who gives the growth."

Affirmations

I think true thoughts under the guidance of the Holy Spirit. I plant seeds of goodness, truth, beauty, and plenty in the soil of my soul.

I trust the living God to bring growth and increase of his kingdom in my mind, body, and affairs. I relax, let go, and let God.

I courageously accept the finished results. I see the best, and I choose the best.

The Wheat and the Tares

²⁴Another parable he put before them, saying, "The king-
dom of heaven may be compared to a man who sowed
good seed in his field; ²⁵but while men were sleeping, his
enemy came and sowed weeds among the wheat, and
went away. ²⁶So when the plants came up and bore grain,
then the weeds appeared also. ²⁷And the servants of the
householder came and said to him, 'Sir, did you not sow
good seed in your field? How then has it weeds?' ²⁸He said
to them, 'An enemy has done this.' The servants said to
him, 'Then do you want us to go and gather them?' ²⁹But
he said, 'No; lest in gathering the weeds you root up the
wheat along with them. ³⁰Let both grow together until the
harvest; and at harvest time {*Thomas:* the weeds will be
plainly visible.} I will tell the reapers, Gather the weeds
first and bind them in bundles to be burned, but gather
the wheat into my barn.'"
   —Matthew 13:24–30 (parallel passage: Thomas 57)

In this parable the kingdom of heaven is likened to a harvest, when the wheat is gathered into the barn and the tares are
burned. The *sower* is again the conscious mind. The *field* is the
subconscious mind; here, however, the meaning includes sub-
liminal contents of both an individual and a collective nature.
Good *seed* are thoughts that are in harmony with the indwelling
Christ—whatever is good and positive and constructive. *Tares*
are negative thoughts and beliefs. *The enemy* is the collective
belief in evil and limitation.
   The weed referred to in this parable is the *lolium temulen-
tum.* Known as the *tare* or *darnel,* it is a grass that resembles
wheat in its earlier stages of growth. In the Near East, a

farmer's enemies sometimes make trouble by throwing tare seeds onto his field. One problem is that the wheat and darnel are hard to tell apart, and many people become dizzy and nauseated if they inadvertently eat darnel. Another is that the roots of the tares grow around the wheat roots. If a farmer pulled up the weeds, he would also uproot much of his wheat.

The farmer's tactics in the parable are correct. The tares only grow to a certain height. After that, it is easy to tell the difference. When the wheat became ripe, he harvested it. By gathering the darnel straw into bundles, he not only got rid of it, but also obtained fuel for cooking and heating. Because of the shortage of trees in Palestine, this makes sense. The man in the parable thus outwitted his enemy in a double sense: he still had a substantial crop of wheat, and he used the tares to his own advantage.

"While men were sleeping," the enemy came and planted the tares. *Sleep* represents a careless, negative, and indifferent attitude. It also represents being ignorant of the divine presence and of the spiritual basis of life. Awakening, by contrast, is a symbol of illumination. For example, Ephesians 5:14 declares:

> Awake, O sleeper, and arise from the dead,
> and Christ shall give you light.

Every person on earth has a mixture of truth and error in his consciousness. The parable, however, teaches that this situation is temporary, and destined to end. Also, if we remain awake and alert to the Divine Presence, we can avoid sowing any more tares. At the same time, the parable advises against pulling out the already existing "weeds" immediately. Jesus' audience knew that if the farmer had pulled up the tares right away, he would also have lost much of his wheat.

It is well to be enthusiastic about spiritual growth, but not over-zealous. A person can be so intent on rooting out what is false from his mind and actions that he also roots out much that is good and helpful. As with the wheat and tares in the parable, the two are hard to tell apart at an early stage of growth. There is also a need to advance beyond a mechanical view of what is *good*, and what is *bad*. These terms can become more of a snare than an aid to understanding. Therefore, patience is needed to allow for the orderly progress of the Spirit's healing action in one's soul. "Let patience have its perfect work, that ye may be perfect and entire, lacking in nothing." (James 1:4, American Standard Version).

Also, there is a great difference between *denial* and *resistance*. On the basis that God is all and God is good, we are to deny evil as a reality, but not to resist it. In the earlier stages of spiritual growth, denial and resistance are easily confused. All things become clear, however, with the orderly growth of understanding.

Emmet Fox explains:

Good is permanent, omnipresent, and all-powerful; and evil [is] a temporary, insubstantial belief, without character of its own, which is destroyed by scientific prayer. Thus, what may be called *the secret of spiritual treatment* is, not to wrestle with the error, which only gives it further life and power, but to destroy it by withdrawing from it just that very energy of belief that gives it its body. *The only existence it has, is that which you give it by temporarily ensouling it with your thought.*[4]

The time of harvest is when we have made clear, conscious contact with God. Then we can easily tell the difference between true ideas and erroneous beliefs. The version in Matthew implies this, but that in Thomas is more specific: "For on the day of the harvest *the weeds will be plainly visible*, and they will be pulled up and burned."

Matthew 13:37–43 gives an interpretation of this parable. It is apparent, however, that this is not from Jesus but from an early church leader, probably the compiler of the gospel of Matthew. Note that the gospel of Thomas includes the parable but no interpretation. This follows the pattern of Mark 4:3–8 and 4:14–20, in that the parable itself is original with Jesus, but not the commentary.

Contrary to the discredited comments in Matthew 13:41–42, the burning of the tares has nothing to do with hellfire and damnation. As Carl G. Jung noted, fire represents an

inner process of transformation.[5] It refers to purification, the
action of God by which mental and emotional weeds are
burned up, and destroyed or transmuted to a higher level. "For
he is like a refiner's fire" (Malachi 3:2). Fire also represents illumination, as in the account of Pentecost: "And there appeared
to them tongues as of fire, distributed and resting on each one
of them" (Acts 2:3). Also, from a Jungian point of view, much
that seems dark and evil in the psyche can be integrated and
transformed into something positive and good. The tares in the
parable, after all, become ultimately useful. As already noted,
when they are gathered and bundled they can be used for cooking and heating.

The day of harvest is truly the day of fulfillment. We reap
the wheat—the positive ideas that we have sown—and gather it
into our barn. The tares—inner factors that seemed to limit our
progress—are redeemed by the fire of Spirit. The kingdom has
come, and God's will has been done, "on earth as it is in heav-
en."

Affirmations

I let patience do its perfect work. I am made consciously
whole and perfect, lacking in nothing.

I do not work with God's ideas to set things right. I work
with God's ideas so that I can see things right.

I am open and receptive to the orderly growth of the
Spirit's healing action within me.

I let go of my personal views of what is good. I let the
mind of Christ instruct me. As I do so, I judge truly between
truth and error in all things.

Chapter 8

The Mustard Seed

[31]Another parable he put before them, saying, "The kingdom of heaven is like a grain of mustard seed which a man
took and sowed in his field; [32]it is the smallest of all seeds,
but when it has grown it is the greatest of shrubs [and
becomes a tree], so that the birds of the air come and
make nests in its branches."   *—Matthew 13:31-32*

The disciples said to Jesus, "Tell us what the kingdom of
heaven is like." He said to them, "It is like a mustard seed.
It is the smallest of all seeds. But when it falls on tilled
soil, it produces a great plant and becomes a shelter for
birds of the sky."
                        —Thomas 20 (parallel passages: Mark 4:30-32;
                                          Luke 13:18-19)

The mustard seed was the smallest seed available in the
ancient Near East. The mustard plant, however, grows to great
size near the Sea of Galilee and the River Jordan. A height of
ten feet is not unusual. Jesus meant to contrast the smallness of
the seed with the bigness of the mature plant. In Jungian psychology, this reflects the archetype of the child, in which a tiny
seed works to fulfill its potential with invincible power. As a
child grows from a single cell to become a man or a woman,
and a mustard seed becomes a large shrub where conditions are
favorable, so it is with the expansion of spiritual consciousness.
Such is the vitality of the Christ consciousness within us to
grow and increase in our awareness.

The mustard seed, then, is a symbol of the remarkable
energy of the indwelling Christ. It begins very small among all
the thoughts in the mind; yet it has enormous potential to

expand until it becomes the dominant power of the soul. The birds, mentioned in all four versions, nest in the plant's shade or in its branches. These birds are images of spiritual ascent. They represent divine ideas that come to permanent awareness, such as love, life, truth, substance, and spirit.

Christ in us is a constant, an organized potential. In the early stages of spiritual growth, however, one needs a firm resolve to focus attention on the Christ within. What we think upon grows. The Christ idea is to become the central point of attention. Introduced in the midst of our often conflicting thoughts and interests, it brings balance and harmony.

Jesus emphasized the active role of the conscious mind in these earlier stages. In Matthew and Luke, a man *took the seed in his hand* and sowed it. In Thomas, the seed falls *on tilled soil,* again pointing to the need for conscious preparation. Then, the more dominant true ideas become, the more they expand in our awareness as a result of their own spontaneous energy and potential. This is like most plants when they are firmly rooted and reach a certain stage of growth—they then keep on growing without much help, if they are given half a chance.

At other times, Jesus used the mustard seed as an image of the expanding power of a quickened faith. He did not mean that a tiny bit of faith can have great results. He did, however, affirm the potential growth of spiritual confidence and trust, and the mighty works that can be released as a result of such an unfoldment. For example, Matthew 17:20 declares (compare Luke 17:5–6): "Truly I say to you, if you have faith as a grain of mustard seed, you will say to this mountain, 'Move from here to there,' and it will move; and nothing will be impossible to you."

Affirmations

I invite the growing consciousness of the Christ mind, my indwelling Lord and Teacher.

I identify with the indwelling Christ and Its ideas. I am whole, complete, and mature in spirit.

True faith and understanding are quickened within me, and radiate through me to establish order and harmony in my world.

Chapter 9

The Leaven

He told them another parable. "The kingdom of heaven
is like leaven which a woman took and hid in three measures of meal, till it was all leavened."
    –Matthew 13:33 (parallel passages: Luke 13:20-21;
                                            Thomas 96)

Leaven is fermented dough, used to raise and lighten
bread; it works the same way as yeast. When the leavened
dough is placed in an oven, the baking bread produces a beautiful aroma and finally food tasty to the mouth and satisfying to
the stomach. Women baked bread daily, and kept some of the
dough aside to use as leaven the next day.

In biblical times, people often referred to leaven in a negative way. This is in keeping with the natural function of molds
and similar life forms. As a symbol, leaven applied to influences
that corrupt the mind and debase character. For example, Jesus
said: "Take heed and beware of the leaven of the Pharisees and
Sadducees" (Matthew 16:6). By this he meant not only the
teachings of these sects, as stated in Matthew 16:12, but also
their dissociation from the subconscious realm of images and
non-verbal symbols. Their obsession with external forms and
ceremonies indicates what we might today call a left-brain fixa-
tion.

Referring to the Passover, Paul reflects the accepted usage
of leaven as a symbol:

Your boasting is not good. Do you not know that a little
leaven leavens the whole lump? Cleanse out the old leaven
that you may be a new lump, as you really are unleavened.
For Christ, our paschal lamb, has been sacrificed. Let us,

therefore, celebrate the festival, not with the old leaven, the
leaven of malice and evil, but with the unleavened bread of
sincerity and truth.

—1 Corinthians 5:6-8

Jesus' parables often took an unexpected turn. The
imagery of this one, however, challenged conventional usage
from the start. Here the leaven does not corrupt, but represents
divine ideas at work to transform the soul in a positive sense
and make it whole. Spirit lifts our consciousness, as leaven
makes the dough rise.

The analogy is close between baker's yeast and action within the human mind and soul. Its work is *invisible* and *silent.* Yet
under the surface, tremendous activity takes place. Leaven
spreads forcefully through the dough, overcomes all resistance,
and finally becomes completely prevalent. Then the attack ceas-
es and peace is restored.

In Jesus' parable, the woman *hid* the leaven. This suggests
the invisible and silent nature of its work. There is unmistak-
able outer evidence, but what we see with our eyes is *the outer
result* of its inward action. The silence of its workings is also significant. Deep meditation is like this, and it is correctly referred
to as *the silence.* To the worldly-minded, things get done where
there is clamor and frenetic activity. Jesus is saying that the
reverse is true. Spiritual causation is silent and invisible, as it
works in the hidden realms of thought, feeling, and belief.

Finally, let us extend this parable to its obvious conclusion.
The bread is baked and then eaten. The bread becomes part of
the cell structure of the people who eat it. In a similar fashion,
divine ideas are assimilated into mind, body, and outer activities. The initial seed thoughts are inwardly processed, and then
incarnated in visible form.

Ervin Seale explains:

If you deal with an idea long enough, that is, meditate
upon it and think about it and around it, you will notice
that the action soon reverses itself. Instead of your dealing
with an idea, the idea is now dealing with you. The polarity
has changed, and instead of the action beginning with you

and impinging upon the idea, the action is now taking place in the idea and it is moving you, and animating you. In this principle is the true science of the mind.[6]

This applies, of course, to corrupting and debasing beliefs. It applies equally, however—and more powerfully—to the indwelling action of the Holy Spirit. Its leaven is love, joy, wisdom, satisfaction, and peace. The true leaven of spiritual consciousness overcomes what is false and negative. We can give full scope to the good and the true, and thus, as Paul said, "be transformed by the renewal of your mind" (Romans 12:2).

Affirmations

I invite the leaven of the Holy Spirit to work in and through me now.

I am renewed in love, joy, wisdom, satisfaction, and peace.

I am transformed by the renewal of my mind.

Chapter 10

The Jar

**Jesus said, "The kingdom of the father is like a certain
woman who was carrying a jar full of meal. While she was
walking on the road, still some distance from home, the
handle of the jar broke and the meal emptied out behind
her on the road. She did not realize it; she had noticed no
accident. When she reached her house, she set the jar
down and found it empty."**

—*Thomas 97*

The parable of the jar, like that of the great fish, is found
only in the gospel of Thomas. We know from a mid-second century work, also found at Nag Hammadi, that the early church
knew of it. *The Gospel of Truth,* a Valentinian writing, compares
two classes of jars. The good jars are filled, supplied, purified,
and made perfect. The bad jars are empty, poured out, broken,
or fit to be smashed. In another passage, this same work states
that the full jars are sealed. It relates the sealing ointment or
pitch to the inspiration of the indwelling Christ. (The word
Christ, a title which means "The Anointed One," fits this symbology.) If the anointing or sealant dissolves, a jar loses its contents.

According to *The Gospel of Truth:*

The anointing is the mercy of the Father with which he will
have mercy on them. And those whom he has anointed,
they are complete. For it is the full jars that are wont to be
anointed. But when the anointing of one jar shall be
destroyed, it is wont to leak. And the reason why it shall
lack content is the fact that its anointing shall depart from
it.[7]

54

In keeping with this commentary, anointing is a basic key to the parable's interpretation. In both the Old and New Testaments, anointing refers to the consciousness and vitality of the indwelling Spirit. The broken handle in the parable implies the loss of the anointing, the loss of spiritual consciousness and vitality in the individual.

The gospel of Thomas links the parable of the leaven (#96) with that of the jar (#97). Jesus probably gave the first parable several times, and at least once followed it with the second. Note the *direct contrast* in the two parables, suggesting an original linkage. In the first, the meal is made into dough and leavened. It is prepared to be baked and eaten. In the second, the meal is gradually and carelessly lost. Nothing nourishing or useful comes of it. Also, in the first, a woman leavens the dough, while in the second, a woman loses the meal.

In the traditional Near East, women often carry jars full of water or meal. Men do not do this kind of work. Thus, when Jesus wanted to convene his apostles for the last supper, he arranged for a *man* to carry a jar of water, who would greet them and take them to the meeting place. This signal worked, because it was so unusual (Mark 14:12–16; Luke 22:7–13).

As in the parable of the leaven, the woman is again a symbol of the soul. She begins her walk—meaning her way of life and thought—with a full jar. At the end, she arrives at her house with an empty jar. The meal, which is milled seed, represents divine ideas. These contents are lost in the course of her walk, but so gradually that she fails to take notice.

Similarly, many children begin life on earth with great promise. Their jar is filled to the brim with potentials of wisdom, love, health, talent, and creativity. Yet as they grow, mature, and make their way in adult life, their progress, like the woman's in the parable, is more apparent than real. Many move further and further away from God's original plan for them. They form mental walls and false limits around themselves, and lose sight of their true capacities. At the end of earth life, they find spiritual growth unattained and hopes unfulfilled. Their jar is empty.

While Jesus' intent is sufficiently clear, there is a paradox implicit in the parable of the jar. In his manner of speaking, he in effect said: "It is the case with the kingdom of the Father as with the woman, even, or especially, when she sets her jar down and finds it empty." This would make no sense to a casual listener. What Jesus implied, however, makes perfect sense. He meant that *the emptiness was apparent rather than real.* The loss of a day's food need not be the end of her world. Much more importantly, if the recognition of the empty jar implied her becoming aware of spiritual emptiness, and with that the need for a new beginning, this could be the most important turning point of her life.

In the realm of outer appearances, a person may be defeated, disgraced, and destitute. Nevertheless, the core of everyone's being, the Christ, is perfect and eternal. Therefore, grace is greater than karma. In a practical sense, this means that a new birth, an inner and outer transformation, is always possible. One's fortunes can yet be restored in every area of life. Even beyond physical death, the soul goes marching on, not to damnation, but to endless opportunities for good.

Affirmations

I am attuned to God's plan for my life. It is a good, a challenging, a positive plan to release the Christ mind within me.

I am a victor in life, not a victim. I prevail over lesser thoughts and attitudes. I know the Christ as my Self, one with God.

I am led in true paths of service. As I give of myself, so do I richly receive from the divine source of all.

Section III–
THE BANQUET
PARABLES

Food, too, is highly symbolic. Religious dietary regula-
tions, such as those of the Catholics, Jews, and
Mohammedans, are observed in order to symbolize
adherence to one's religion. Specific foods are used to
symbolize specific festivals and observances in almost
every country.... And eating together has been a highly
symbolic act throughout all of man's known history:
"companion" means one with whom you share your
bread.[1]

–S.I. Hayakawa

The feasts of the Bible are symbolic. Some really happened and others did not, but this is beside the point. In
Chapter 4, we referred briefly to an actual feast of Jesus and his
disciples. They ate and drank as a dramatic parable of the presence, the nowness, of the kingdom of God. Others wanted
them to fast and to recite traditional prayers, but Jesus declared
through his own actions and those of his students that the time
for sorrow and penitence is past. God offers his messianic feast
of divine ideas, the table is set, and all are invited. The theme
of the *wedding feast*, where used, adds the emphasis of the soul
being wedded to its supreme ideal, the indwelling Christ.

Jesus' feast also reminded people that a joyful God is part
of the truth of our Creator. God is life, health, and joy. The
temple worship involved singing and the use of musical instru-
ments. The liturgical year included Passover, itself a dramatic
symbol of liberation, and other festive events. Thus, as joy is
basic to the divine nature, he and his disciples did not go about

57

with a dour expression. They feasted, danced, and celebrated in the context of the divine presence.

The antiquity of the bread symbol, while by no means limited to the Israelites, is reflected in their early practices. They brought twelve fresh loaves of unleavened bread to the temple every sabbath. These they placed before the holy of holies as a thank offering. The loaves were appropriately called the bread of the Presence. "And you shall set the bread of the Presence on the table before me always" (Exodus 25:30).

Eating the bread of communion is a basic Christian sacrament. The full meaning of the last supper, with its great diversity of interpretations, will never be exhausted. Yet this act of sharing, of breaking bread together, has a deep symbolic significance. Jesus used the occasion to release a consciousness of spiritual oneness, of divine love, within his apostles. All, except Judas, joined in the realization of the I AM, the universal Christ, the bread of life. They knew, not merely believed, that they were sons of God.

To review all the biblical banquets in depth, with their wide range of meaning, would require a book in itself. Within the scope of the present volume are five banquet parables attributed to Jesus. The four that appear to be genuine reflect a recurrent theme: It is God's nature to give of himself fully, but the individual is often unwilling to receive. We are reminded of Richard Trench's statement: "Prayer is not the overcoming of God's reluctance; it is laying hold of His highest willingness."

═══════════════

Chapter 11

The Great Supper

¹⁶But he said to him, "A man once gave a great banquet, and invited many; ¹⁷ and at the same time for the banquet he sent his servant to say to those who had been invited, 'Come; for all is now ready.' ¹⁸But they all alike began to make excuses. The first said to him, 'I have bought a field, and I must go out and see it; I pray you, have me excused.' ¹⁹And another said, 'I have bought five yoke of oxen, and I go to examine them; I pray you, have me excused.' ²⁰And another said, 'I have married a wife, and therefore I cannot come.' ²¹So the servant came and reported this to his master. [Then the householder in anger said to his servant, 'Go out quickly to the streets and lanes of the city, and bring in the poor and maimed and blind and lame.' ²²And the servant said, 'Sir, what you commanded has been done, and still there is room.'] ²³And the master said to the servant, 'Go out to the highways and hedges, and compel people to come in, that my house may be filled. ²⁴[For I tell you, none of those men who were invited shall taste my banquet.]' "

—Luke 14:16–24

Jesus said, "A man had received visitors. And when he had prepared the dinner, he sent his servant to invite the guests. He went to the first one and said to him, 'My master invites you.' He said, 'I have claims against some merchants. They are coming to me this evening. I must go and give them my orders. I ask to be excused from the dinner.' He went to another and said to him, 'My master has invited you.' He said to him, 'I have just bought a house and am required for the day. I shall not have any spare time.' He went to another and said to him, 'My master invites you.' He said to him, 'My friend is going to get

**married, and I am to prepare the banquet. I shall not be
able to come. I ask to be excused from the dinner.' He
went to another and said to him, 'My master invites you.'
He said to him, 'I have just bought a farm, and I am on
my way to collect the rent. I shall not be able to come. I
ask to be excused.' The servant returned and said to his
master, 'Those whom you invited to the dinner have
asked to be excused.' The master said to his servant, 'Go
outside to the streets and bring back those whom you
happen to meet, so that they may dine. [Businessmen and
merchants will not enter the places of my father.]' "**
                —Thomas 64 (parallel passage: Matthew 22:1-10)

The parable of the great supper exists in three versions.
Apparently there was a single source underlying Matthew
22:1-10 and Luke 14:16-24. While Thomas 64 carries the same
essential meanings, however, Jesus probably spoke it at a different time and place. The following facts point to this conclusion:

First, the four excuses listed in Thomas 64 are all different
from the three in Luke 14:16-24.

Second, the version in Luke points to a rural setting, while
that in Thomas is more urban in character. For example, in
Luke one man uses the excuse that he bought a field and must
go out to see it. Another bought five yoke of oxen, and must go
to look at them. In Thomas, one man has a claim against some
merchants who are coming to see him that evening. Another
bought a farm (some translators say a whole village) as a real
estate investment, and is on the way to collect the rent. There is
a strong presumption, then, that Jesus adapted the parable to
two audiences.

Third, some scholars have noted that in folk tales, sets of
three usually predominate; this does not, however, carry over to
the parables of Jesus which are a different genre. Also, in a
broader sense, both three and four were widely used in ancient
symbology. For example, Revelation 21 pictures the new
Jerusalem as having four walls, with three gates each. The zodiac has twelve signs, but there are four types of sign (earth, air,
fire, and water) and three signs of each type. The use of twelve,
also prominent, utilizes the fact that 3x4=12. In addition, 3+4=7,

the most prominent number in biblical numerology which, in turn, correlates with seven heavenly bodies: the sun, the moon, and the planets Mercury, Venus, Mars, Jupiter, and Saturn. The ancients had no telescopes, and thus no knowledge of Uranus, Neptune, or Pluto.

Carl G. Jung also gave equal weight to triads (sets of three) and tetrads (sets of four) in their symbolic significance.[2] He specifically related the number four to psychic wholeness, which "plays a considerable role in the picture-world of the unconscious."[3]

Except for the number and exact nature of the excuses, which differ, all three versions have a similar literary structure. By noting this pattern, we can clarify the original form of the parable recorded in Matthew 22:1–10/Luke 14:16–24. We will interpret from the Lucan text; by removing two interpolations we come close to the original wording. The version in Matthew is further from the original, and has special features to be discussed in Chapter 15.

Note that all three versions have different endings. Matthew attaches the parable of the wedding robe (22:11–13) to that of the great supper, thus combining two completely separate parables. Luke 14:24 reads: "For I tell you, none of those men who were invited shall taste my banquet." This is unnecessary, since the invited guests had already made known their decision not to attend. The final sentence in Thomas, with respect to businessmen and merchants, is also secondary. Jesus did not oppose business and merchandising, honorably conducted. As these three endings are entirely unlike each other, and all fit awkwardly into their respective texts, they were not part of the original context and should be disregarded.

Also, after the refusal of the invited guests, Matthew 22:9 reads: "Go therefore to the thoroughfares, and invite to the marriage feast as many as you find." The parallel passage in Thomas states: "Go outside to the streets and bring back those whom you happen to meet, so that they may dine." Luke, however, has the servant go out *twice* to find attenders from among the public at large. As a result, the parable can now be stretched a bit to carry a meaning quite apart from what Jesus intended.

The enlarged text includes three categories of people: (1) the invited guests; (2) the poor and maimed and blind and lame; and (3) those found in the highways and hedges.

According to Luke's modified text, *the invited guests* may be seen as the religious authorities in Jerusalem, who had refused Jesus and his gospel. The *poor, maimed, blind, and lame* are probably the poor and oppressed among the Jewish people, though other conclusions are possible. *Those found in the highways and hedges* may be seen as the Gentiles. Jesus, it is true, invited everyone to join him at the Father's table. He did not, however, plan this specific parable for the purpose that the later editor had in mind. As Joachim Jeremias concludes:

> Since Matthew (22.9f.) and the Gospel of Thomas (64) refer to only *one* invitation to the uninvited, the double invitation will be an expansion of the parable....to him [Luke] the introduction of the Gentiles into the Kingdom of God was of the first importance. It was the Church in a situation demanding missionary activity, which interpreted the parable as a missionary command.[4]

One additional point needs to be made. Luke 14:23, which is part of the original parable, is translated "*compel* people to come in." In the history of the church, Christian leaders have sometimes used this passage to justify forced conversions. The original context, however, shows this to have been a mistake. George Lamsa, who spent his early years in the Near East, comments on 14:23 as follows:

> The Aramaic word *alesso* [translated "compel" in English] means urge and insist. An Oriental host almost begs his guests to attend saying, "You must come to my house. By the head of my son I would not eat if you are not present. My house is your house. I am your servant." Such urgency is due to the fact that no banquet is a success unless the house is crowded and there is a waiting line of guests outside. Such a full attendance advertises the popularity of the host.[5]

At Oriental banquets, then, a host who did not have a

house full of guests would "lose face." The host could not *compel* anyone to attend, i.e. he would not be in a position to send out ruffians or use physical force. He would, however, *urge* people to come and eat. It was considered polite to initially decline such an invitation, even if asked several times. Finally, the invited person would accept. Luke 14:23, then, cannot be validly used in support of forced conversions.

Based on Luke 14:16–21a, 23, we find a parable that can be viewed in more than one way. Different clusters of meaning unfold, depending upon whom we consider the master of the feast to be. Nor can we say that one approach is right and the other is wrong; both are valid starting points.

If the reader identifies the master of the feast with God, we are taught the following: God offers his feast of divine ideas, which supplies every human need. What is more, we don't have a Creator who is distant and aloof, begrudging his gifts to us. Rather, *divine love seeks us out by issuing the invitations.* Stated another way, the indwelling Spirit ever impinges upon our consciousness, seeking to reconcile our inner world (and, indirectly, our outer world) with itself.

On the surface, the excuses of the invited guests make sense. They reflect valid interests—of home, wife, farm, and business. Yet they involve purely temporal concerns, which effectively keep the invited ones away from the feast. As Elizabeth Boyden Howes observes, "It is not that response to the supranatural is good and concern for the natural is bad. Rather, it is a question of appropriateness and timing."[6]

Jesus understood that outer accumulation, when pursued at the expense of inner development, is an illusory goal. He realized that even regarding "material" things, a person's security is not in outer resources but in conscious oneness with God. As he said at another time: "Seek first his kingdom and his righteousness, and all these things shall be yours as well" (Matthew 6:33).

There is, however, a second way that a reader can enter the world of this parable. One can identify not with any of the guests, but with the master of the feast. In real life, the failure of one or two guests to come would not be too strange, but for none to come would be a negative miracle. The central meaning of this is that the host's former continuity of things is rudely interrupted. This is similar to the individual whose former sense of material cause and effect is shattered, and replaced by a new and truer vision of how the universe works.

This radical change of perception is inherent to the parable form as Jesus used it. It teaches the basic law: *As within, so without.* In so doing, it upsets our former ways of thinking and getting things done. Nevertheless, it is the way—indeed, the *only* way—that we can fully accept the good that God has for us. The hearer is therefore confronted with a choice: He can cling to the illusion that he is separated from God, and that contrary forces are blocking his progress. Or he can, *through an inward attunement,* confidently receive the blessings of the kingdom, and show them forth in every area of life. No one, however, can do both at the same time. Each individual must either accept, or deny, the fact that the way to God's good is open. There is no middle ground here, and no way to serve two masters.

As a final point, we should note that many people have reviewed this parable's excuses in detail, and have found specific meanings in each one. (Of course, with the discovery of Thomas' version, the number of excuses available for this purpose has increased from three to seven.) This is a valid procedure, as long as we remember that the excuses are intentionally open-ended, and will carry different shades of meaning for different interpreters. Also, meanings will shift for the same individual at different times.

Affirmations

I attend my Father's great banquet, the feast of infinite ideas that are my divine inheritance.

The way to my good is always open. The indwelling Christ is the open door that no one can shut.

I am open and receptive to the truth. I am ready to view the earth and its laws in a new way.

I claim my innate dominion within the laws of the kingdom of God.

Chapter 12

The Chief Seats

> [7]Now he told a parable to those who were invited, when he marked how they chose the places of honor, saying to them, [8]"When you are invited by any one to a marriage feast, do not sit down in a place of honor, lest a more eminent man than you be invited by him; [9]and he who invited you both will come and say to you, 'Give place to this man,' and then you will begin with shame to take the lowest place. [10]But when you are invited, go and sit in the lowest place, so that when your host comes he may say to you, 'Friend, go up higher'; then you will be honored in the presence of all who sit at table with you. [11]For every one who exalts himself will be humbled, and he who humbles himself will be exalted."   *–Luke 14:7–11*

The ancient Jews gave great weight to protocol, including seating arrangements. Protocol is still a factor in modern life, but not with the same intensity of concern. The literary background of this parable is Proverbs 25:6–7:

> Do not put yourself forward in the king's presence
> or stand in the place of the great;
> for it is better to be told, "Come up here,"
> than to be put lower in the presence of the prince.

Many of the statements at the end of Jesus' parables do not belong to their original context. In this instance, however, 14:11 almost certainly did originally follow 14:7–10. In 14:11, Jesus paraphrased the Rabbi Hillel who said:

> My abasement is my exaltation,
> and my exaltation is my abasement.

Hillel (approx. 60 BC-20 A.D.), an older contemporary of Jesus, was a teacher of real stature. His name is still honored in the Jewish tradition. Jesus no doubt knew of him and his work, and perhaps knew him personally. The golden rule, given in Matthew 7:12, restates in a positive way what Hillel had said negatively: "What you hate, do not do to your fellow man. This is the whole law; all else is commentary." This, in turn, expands Tobit 4:15: "What you hate, do not do to any one."

A later rabbi, Simeon ben Azzai (approx. 110 A.D.), drew both from Hillel and Jesus. He offered somewhat similar advice on table manners: "Stand two or three places below your proper place and wait, until they say to you, 'Come up here.' " Then, as authority, ben Azzai quoted Hillel's statement on abasement and exaltation. This later teacher thus missed the central meaning of Jesus' parable—which we shall discuss shortly—and took his words merely as advice on proper etiquette.

Returning to our text, the narrative begins: "He marked how they chose the places of honor." This is a polite way of saying that the guests argued over, and perhaps scrambled for, the "best" seats, meaning those that carried a higher rank. They had probably acted in an uncouth way, unbecoming to their station in life. Also, the man deprived of a good seat would end up with the lowest rank. The other guests would not have each moved down a notch to make room for him.

Jesus meant that *there are two ways to make progress in life.* One is by striving and struggling in competition with other people. Those who vied for the "best" seats at the banquet table are like those who, through worldly wits if not physical force, fight to obtain wealth and position. In this game, for whatever it is worth, there have to be winners and losers. A few make it to the top, while others fall to the bottom. This whole attitude weakens the fabric of society, depresses the economy, and turns life into a struggle for existence. So even those who win lose; they exalt themselves and are humbled, failing to find true satisfaction in life.

The other way to succeed and make progress is less direct, but far more effective in the long run. A person makes a mental picture of what he wants to achieve, focuses on that image or series of images, and allows the law of creative consciousness to work. As Emmet Fox put it, he builds *a mental equivalent* of his goals.

This process often leads to diligent efforts in the outer world. Its primary focus, though, is on inward attunement. It is like the man who chose the "lowest" place, maintained a relaxed attitude, and then was invited to occupy a seat of honor. And one of the best features is that everyone can be a winner, and no one need be a loser. We are all born to win, to successfully fulfill our God-given capacities and goals. As Luke 14:11 implies, everyone who humbles himself to the creative law—AS WITHIN, SO WITHOUT—releasing its energy in positive ways, will be exalted.

Affirmations

I humble myself to the laws of the kingdom. I accept the fact that the laws of thought are the laws of destiny.

I joyfully receive God's whole and perfect plan for my life. I joyfully work with that plan in thought, word, and action, and I am exalted.

I joyfully let all others accept God's whole and perfect plan for their lives.

I joyfully assist them in achieving these plans, in ways that, and to the extent that, the Holy Spirit guides me to do so.

Chapter 13

The Ten Virgins

[1]"Then the kingdom of heaven shall be compared to ten maidens who took their lamps and went to meet the bridegroom. [2]Five of them were foolish, and five were wise. [3]For when the foolish took their lamps, they took no oil with them; [4]but the wise took flasks of oil with their lamps. [5]As the bridegroom was delayed, they all slumbered and slept. [6]But at midnight there was a cry, 'Behold, the bridegroom! Come out to meet him.' [7]Then all those maidens rose and trimmed their lamps. [8]And the foolish said to the wise, 'Give us some of your oil, for our lamps are going out.' [9]But the wise replied, 'Perhaps there will not be enough for us and for you; go rather to the dealers and buy for yourselves.' [10]And while they went to buy, the bridegroom came, and those who were ready went in with him to the marriage feast; and the door was shut. [[11]Afterward the other maidens came also, saying, 'Lord, lord, open to us.' [12]But he replied, 'Truly, I say to you, I do not know you.' [13]Watch therefore, for you know neither the day nor the hour.]"

—Matthew 25:1–13

This parable reflects actual wedding customs of ancient Palestine. Joachim Jeremias noted that the same bridal customs are still followed in modern Palestine. This includes receiving the bridegroom with lamps, and the delay in his arrival until after dark.[7] George Lamsa, on the basis of first-hand experience, furnished similar data. In his discussion of the lamps, he wrote:

The parents of the bridegroom, neighbors, friends and strangers, provide abundant light for the wedding night.

Light is a symbol of happiness and no wedding is properly conducted without plenty of light.[8]

He also confirmed that after the arrival of the bridegroom and his party, and the entry of the guests into the house, the door is locked. Even if latecomers knock and someone hears them, they will be kept out if there is too little space inside.

The original parable, however, ended with the locked door in verse 10. Verses 11–13 are a later addition, made to relate the text to the hoped-for second coming of Christ. According to this reinterpretation, the personal Jesus becomes the bridegroom. Believers must keep themselves ready for his return to earth in glory. The wise virgins are the persons accepted into his kingdom. The foolish virgins are those who are kept out.

The secondary nature of 25:11–13 is clear for the following reasons:

(1) When Jesus gave the parable, he was still obviously living on earth. Therefore, his giving a parable to illustrate a *second* coming is unlikely. He had not yet left the *first* time, and the events that made a second coming plausible—including his resurrection—had not yet occurred.

(2) Verses 11–12 resemble Luke 13:25, which occurs in a collection of sayings unattached to our parable. These two readings, then, are variants of a common tradition drawn upon by both gospel writers. Luke 13:22–30, shown in Crossan's Workbook, is not a parable but a composite which links together several oral traditions.

(3) Verse 13 declares: "Watch therefore, for you know neither the day nor the hour." This also fails to fit the context. For the parable does not state that five girls stayed awake, and the others did not. In fact, all ten of them fell asleep (25:5). The text states, rather, that five of them had enough oil for their lamps, and the others did not. An interpretation, to be valid, must fit the content of the parable itself.

From a literary standpoint, it is the case with the kingdom of heaven as with the parable's end result, which is *joining the marriage feast*. In essence, the kingdom is the mystical union of the soul with God. This is also the true goal of our existence. In

a symbolic sense, it is what the wedding guests came to celebrate.[9]

The five foolish maidens are the outer senses of sight,
hearing, smell, taste, and touch. They have valid functions on
the earth plane, but their weakness is a tendency to fragment
experience. These, however, have spiritual counterparts—the
five wise maidens—which give insights not available to the other
five. For example, Jesus declared on various occasions:
"Whoever has ears to hear, let him hear." There is a spiritual
receptivity of which the visible ear is only a symbol.

In the parable, the five wise virgins can enter the wedding
feast because they have their lamps ready with oil. This means
that the spiritual senses can enter the consciousness of oneness,
because they have the light of understanding. The five foolish
virgins lack oil in their lamps, and cannot enter. That is, the five
material senses are kept out because of their inherent limitations.

Many Bible passages point to a symbolic lamp which
inspires the mind and illumines the understanding. For example:

> Yea, thou dost light my lamp;
> > the Lord my God lightens my darkness.
> > > > —Psalm 18:28

> Thy word is a lamp to my feet
> > and a light to my path.
> > > > —Psalm 119:105

> The spirit of man is the lamp of the Lord,
> > searching all his innermost parts.
> > > > —Proverbs 20:27

Anointing with oil is another symbol of divine inspiration.
A classic example is Psalm 23, in which the shepherd pours
refreshing olive oil over his weary sheep's head: "Thou anoin-
test my head with oil, my cup overflows" (Psalm 23:5). The messianic prophecy in Isaiah 61 includes a passage which extols the

granting of "the oil of gladness instead of mourning" (Isaiah 61:3).

The New Testament also refers to anointing. For example, Peter proclaimed "how God anointed Jesus of Nazareth with the Holy Spirit and with power" (Acts 10:38). The word *Christ*, as stated in Chapter 10, itself means "The Anointed One." Also, Paul declared:

> If you and we belong to Christ, guaranteed as his and anointed, it is all God's doing; it is God also who has set his seal upon us, and as a pledge of what is to come has given the Spirit to dwell in our hearts.
>
> —2 Corinthians 1:21–22 (NEB)

The need, then, is to obtain oil for our lamps, and not to delay in doing so. Meditation and other spiritual disciplines are essential. They are needed if we hope to consciously unite with our own highest Self, the Christ. We can delay our spiritual progress, like the foolish girls who came with too little oil. The natural result, however, is to lose our chance to advance toward fulfillment in all areas—not forever, but for a long time to come. We are warned, in effect, not just to talk about the laws of creative consciousness, but to *actually practice* them in a positive way, day in and day out.

At the same time, we have the assurance that those who are spiritually prepared will be admitted to the wedding feast. The prepared ones give prominent attention to the central reality, the one Mind, the one presence and power in whom we live, move, and have our being. They are married to their own highest Self, the Christ. The inner and the outer aspects of their being are no longer in conflict, but continue in a harmonious flow from Spirit to soul to body and environment. In the imagery of Jesus' parable, their lamps are lit, their oil is sufficient, and the door is open to them.

Affirmations

I give attention to the one Mind, the one presence and power in whom I live, move, and have my being.

I yield my soul to the greater realization of the Christ. I am wed to my own highest ideal.

Through the Christ, I am in the Father, and the Father is in me.

I am alive and awake to the indwelling ideas that are the substance of all form. I claim the good that is mine under divine law.

Chapter 14

The Rich Man and Lazarus

[19]"There was a rich man, who was clothed in purple and fine linen and who feasted sumptuously every day. [20]And at his gate lay a poor man named Lazarus, full of sores, [21]who desired to be fed with what fell from the rich man's table; moreover the dogs came and licked his sores. [22]The poor man died and was carried by the angels to Abraham's bosom. The rich man also died and was buried; [23]and in Hades, being in torment, he lifted up his eyes, and saw Abraham far off and Lazarus in his bosom. [24]And he called out, 'Father Abraham, have mercy upon me, and send Lazarus to dip the end of his finger in water and cool my tongue; for I am in anguish in this flame.' [25]But Abraham said, 'Son, remember that you in your lifetime received your good things, and Lazarus in like manner evil things; but now he is comforted here, and you are in anguish. [26]And besides all this, between us and you a great chasm has been fixed, in order that those who would pass from here to you may not be able, and none may cross from there to us.' [27]And he said, 'Then I beg you, Father, to send him to my father's house, [28]for I have five brothers, so that he may warn them, lest they also come into this place of torment.' [29]But Abraham said, 'They have Moses and the prophets; let them hear them.' [30]And he said, 'No, Father Abraham; but if some one goes to them from the dead, they will repent.' [31]He said to him, 'If they do not hear Moses and the prophets, neither will they be convinced if some one should rise from the dead.'"   *–Luke 16:19–31*

The story of the rich man and Lazarus is based on an Egyptian folk tale. The Jews adapted this story in various ways,

73

and Luke records one version of it. Its wide departure from
Jesus' pattern of teaching makes his use of it unlikely. Contrary
to his parables in general it does not, in its outer sense, deal
with everyday things. Rather, it takes Lazarus and Dives (the
rich man's name in tradition) to Hades, which was the Greek
conception of the afterlife and contained both pleasant and
unpleasant places. Also, Dives converses with Abraham.

Joachim Jeremias, commenting on Luke 16:19–26, states:

> The first part derives from well-known folk-material con-
> cerned with the reversal of fortune in the after life. This is
> the Egyptian folk-tale of the journey Si-Osiris, the son of
> Setme Chamois to the under-world, which concludes with
> the words: 'He who has been good on earth, will be blessed
> in the kingdom of the dead, and he who has been evil on
> earth, will suffer in the kingdom of the dead.' Alexandrian
> Jews brought this story to Palestine, where it became very
> popular as the story of the poor scholar and the rich publi-
> can Bar Ma'jan.[10]

As a literary form, the rich man and Lazarus is somewhere
between a fable and an allegory. Jesus, it is true, used allegories
in John 10:1–5 and 15:1–10. In these cases, however, the central
motif is the I AM or Christ, viewed in both an indwelling and a
cosmic sense. As the indwelling Christ, I AM is the good shepherd (John 10:11,14), who shepherds the thoughts of the mind.
In a cosmic sense, I AM is the vine (John 15:1–10), in which the
branches (individual souls) bear fruit. Our story cannot be
applied in this way. Whatever value it has will be found along
different lines of inquiry.

George Lamsa attributed the tale to the Oriental imagination, not specifically to Jesus. His comments, with respect to
this story, deal with the obvious and are convincing:

> The parable of Lazarus and the wicked man is based on the
> imagination of the Easterners, who protest and seek
> vengeance in their hearts against the evils of the rich. On
> this earth they can do nothing against a rich man, and have
> to be satisfied with the hope of justice in the hereafter.
> They picture the man who had plenty on this earth and

who had unjustly confiscated their property, as facing star-
vation and punishment in the other world, where the poor
would at last be blessed with abundance.[11]

Other twentieth century interpreters have looked for additional meanings in our text, and this too is valid.[12] The fact that
the Bible includes it is, in itself, important; but just *how*, or *in
what sense*, important is a question that each reader must decide
for himself.

Certainly the story of Lazarus and Dives accords with the
basic intuition that life is ultimately just, even where it seems
unfair. Christianity, Judaism, Hinduism, and Buddhism all
teach a law of cause and effect, in which we reap what we sow in
thought and action. The religions articulate this point differently, but all agree that cause and effect function in a moral sense.
If this process does not complete itself in the present life, it nevertheless will in the future. There are hidden laws of justice
that, though they grind slowly, grind exceedingly small.

The final verse also rings true: "If they do not hear Moses
and the prophets, neither will they be convinced if some one
should rise from the dead." This, like the footpath in the parable of the sower, typifies the dogmatic attitude. Such people are
found not only in religious circles, but in scientific ones as well.
To this day, the rigid dogmatist is the foe of free inquiry and
progress in all walks of life.

Chapter 15

The Wedding Robe

[¹And again Jesus spoke to them in parables, saying,]
²"The kingdom of heaven may be compared to a king who
gave a marriage feast for his son, [³and sent his servants
to call those who were invited to the marriage feast; but
they would not come. ⁴Again he sent other servants, saying, 'Tell those who are invited, Behold, I have made
ready my dinner, my oxen and my fat calves are killed,
and everything is ready; come to the marriage feast.' ⁵But
they made light of it and went off, one to his farm, another to his business {⁶while the rest seized his servants,
treated them shamefully, and killed them. ⁷The king was
angry, and he sent his troops and destroyed those mur-
derers and burned their city}. ⁸Then he said to his servants, 'The wedding is ready, but those invited were not
worthy. ⁹Go therefore to the thoroughfares, and invite to
the marriage feast as many as you find.' ¹⁰And those servants went out into the streets and gathered all whom
they found, both bad and good; so the wedding hall was
filled with guests.] ¹¹But when the king came in to look at
the guests, he saw there a man who had no wedding garment; ¹²and he said to him, 'Friend, how did you get in
here without a wedding garment?' And he was speechless.
¹³Then the king said to the attendants, 'Bind him hand
and foot, and cast him into the outer darkness; there men
will weep and gnash their teeth.' [¹⁴For many are called,
but few are chosen."   *–Matthew 22:1-14*

Here we find an example of the length to which some
early Church leaders were prepared to go in rearranging Jesus'
words to try to meet a changed situation. The author of
Matthew modified the parable of the great supper, reviewed in

Chapter 11, with definite goals in mind. That the parable of the wedding robe was originally separate becomes clear by comparing the versions in Luke and Thomas; these lack any equivalent to Matthew 22:2, 11–13.

As it now stands, Matthew 22:1–14 has some additional problems. In Matthew the host is a king; in Luke and Thomas he is a private citizen. When a king or queen invites someone to a banquet, it amounts to a command. The invited guests would not, acting as a group, dare to refuse such an invitation. For them to abuse, or even kill, the servants bringing the invitations is completely unthinkable. Also, it is patently absurd for the king to have sent out his troops to destroy the offenders and burn their city, while the food got cold on the table.

The absurdity disappears, however, when we recognize verses 6–7 as an interpolation, adapted from yet another parable, that of the wicked husbandmen in Matthew 21:33–41.

The gospel of Matthew, compiled after the fall of Jerusalem, here implies views current in the late first century. Quite frankly, the material has been reworked to yield meanings remote from those intended by Jesus.[13] The editor's point of view was approximately as follows:

Verse	Image	Reinterpreted Meaning
22:2	the king's son	Jesus
22:3	first group of servants	the Old Testament prophets
	invited guests	Jewish religious authorities
22:4	other servants	Jesus' apostles and missionaries (sent to Jerusalem)
22:5-6	servants killed	martyred apostles and missionaries (sent to Jerusalem)
	invited guests	Jewish religious authorities
22:7	punitive expedition	destruction of Jerusalem (70 A.D.)
22:8–9	invited guests	Gentile Christians
22:10	entry into hall	Christian baptism
22:11	inspection of guests	the last judgment
22:13	outer darkness	hell

To recover the original sense of the parable of the wedding robe, we shall ignore this elaborate reconstruction and return to the parable's original form, disregarding all but Matthew 22:2, 11–13. There may have been other material that really belonged between Matthew 22:2 and 22:11, but this is no longer available. Also, verse 14 does not fit the original context, for it declares that *many* are called and *few* are chosen. The original parable, to the contrary, mentions *only one* guest who is ejected from the feast; it makes no mention of multiple rejects.

Turning then to the interpretation, we consider that guests at a wedding are expected to wear clothes that are clean and in good condition. That is true in every culture, east and west. In the Near East, however, people tend to make a heavy emotional investment in matters of protocol, which are ignored at a person's peril.

Bible students have asked: "How can someone be blamed for wearing improper clothes, when one is invited on the spot and not given time to change?" This is a valid question, which can best be answered in the context of the times.

There are two possible explanations. First, in the traditional Near East, some people were too poor to own dress-up clothes. They could, however, readily borrow a clean robe from a well-to-do friend or neighbor. It was the custom to help out in this way, when needed. So the man did not have a valid excuse for coming without proper attire.

On the other hand, it was not unusual for a man of means, when sending out invitations through his servants, to furnish each guest with a special garment for the occasion. There would then be no question of a guest borrowing clothes from a third party, or failing to do so. This second option is more probable. For a king, who gave a marriage feast for his son, would be most unlikely to invite guests from the poorest economic class.

As the case may be, the guest gives his king a double insult. He wears an unfit robe, and refuses to answer the king when asked about it. As a result, he is bound hand and foot, and thrown out into the night.

In Chapter 4, we considered how old and new garments

typify states of consciousness. In the parable, the man could not expect to wear a dirty, worn-out robe and join the wedding feast. This points to the need to let go of old images of sin, disease, lack, and separation. In order to prepare himself, the guest should have taken off his old garment, and put on a clean one. The new garment is the vision of the universe in its spiritual oneness, whole and complete in God. The *wedding* garment, further, emphasizes the soul's union with the indwelling Christ.

The new garment, then, is a transformed consciousness. This imagery has archetypal roots; it is found both in and out of the Bible. For example, the book of Isaiah mentions both the old and the new:

> We have all become like one who is unclean,
>> and all our righteous deeds are like a polluted garment.
>
> —Isaiah 64:6
>
> I will greatly rejoice in the Lord,
>> my soul shall exult in my God;
>> for he has clothed me with the garments of salvation,
>> he has covered me with the robe of righteousness,
>> as a bridegroom decks himself with a garland,
>> and as a bride adorns herself with her jewels.
>
> —Isaiah 61:10

God, the one Mind, is the source of all true ideas and all wisdom. He alone can give the new garment of true understanding. This is another reason for believing that, in this parable's original form, the king himself issued the wedding garments. It fits the essential meaning more closely than the other option, which would have some of the guests borrow clothes from their friends and neighbors.

The old garment, at its core, is a false sense of duality and separation. One can hold on to an illusory belief system if one wishes, but with grave consequences. The man in the parable is bound hand and foot, and thrown into outer darkness. In brief, the bound hand points to an inability to bring one's thoughts and desires to fulfillment. The bound foot is a belief system that is limited to surface appearances. One is prevented from standing upon a consciousness of truth. The outer darkness is a state of ignorance in which we are cut off from the deeper levels of our own being, which seek to make us whole. The weeping and gnashing of teeth—which occurs seven times in the gospels, but still accords well with the original context—pictures intense emotional anguish.

The new garment, by contrast, is a consciousness of wholeness and oneness. As David Bohm, a prominent physicist, explains:

> If one can include everything coherently and harmoniously in an over-all whole that is undivided, unbroken and without a border...then his mind will tend to move in a similar way, and from this will flow an orderly action within the whole.[14]

Whenever, then, we give up an old illusion, gain a new insight, or realize the divine presence more clearly, we are shedding the dirty garment and putting on the clean, white one. This imagery can thus inspire us again and again. Of those who have washed their symbolic robes, and made them white, the book of Revelation declares:

> Therefore are they before the throne of God,
>> and serve him day and night within his temple;
>> and he who sits upon the throne
>> will shelter them in his presence.
>> They shall hunger no more, neither thirst any more;
>> the sun shall not strike them, nor any scorching heat.
>> For the Lamb in the midst of the throne will be their shepherd,
>> and he will guide them to springs of living water;
>> and God will wipe away every tear from their eyes.
>> —Revelation 7:15–17

Affirmations

I throw off the old garment of error, duality, and separation.

I receive the new garment of conscious oneness with God.

I visualize myself as whole and complete in God. I am in the Father, and the Father is in me.

I visualize_____as whole and complete in God. _____is in the Father, and the Father is in_____.

I visualize every man, woman, and child as whole and complete in God.

I visualize the earth as whole and complete in God.

I visualize the universe as whole and complete in God.

I celebrate the wedding of my soul with the indwelling Christ.

Section IV—
THE SERVANT PARABLES

Your present problem is your great opportunity. Your own mind—the Secret Place, as Jesus called it—is the council chamber where the arrangements and decisions for your whole life are made; it is also the drafting room where the plans for your destiny are formed. Your life is your laboratory. The world is your workshop.[1]

—*Emmet Fox*

As modern scholars state, the parables have a double historical setting. First, Jesus presented them at a given time and place. Afterward, the church used them over a period of decades. When they came to be written down, and finally appeared in the gospels, they often assumed meanings quite different from those intended by Jesus.

After his resurrection, many early Christians believed that Jesus would personally return as the Messiah, and preside over a final judgment. Millions of present-day Christians still believe this. The parables, when he gave them, had nothing to do with these concepts. At a later time, however, certain people amended many of them to fit their own expectations.

The servant parables lend themselves to being reworked in this way. Most of them mention, or at least imply, a time of reckoning. Their basic intent, though, is a variation of the harvest theme found in the seed parables. States of consciousness produce definite results in the body and in outer conditions. Both the harvest theme, and that of reckoning, refer to the results of the formative power of thought. As such, the seed parables help us to understand the servant parables.

Despite the contexts into which these parables have sometimes been forced, many readers have intuitively sensed much of their meaning. For example, the doorkeeper's basic point (Mark 13:33–37) has been stated in a nutshell: "Stand porter at the door of your mind." Textual analysis confirms that this is a more plausible interpretation than "wait all night for Jesus to appear."

Chapter 16

The Doorkeeper

³³"Take heed, watch; [for you do not know when the time will come.] ³⁴It is like a man [going on a journey,] when he leaves home [and puts his servants in charge, each with his work,] and commands the doorkeeper to be on the watch. ³⁵Watch therefore—for you do not know when the master of the house will come, in the evening, or at midnight, or at cockcrow, or in the morning—³⁶lest he come suddenly and find you asleep. ³⁷[And what I say to you I say to all: Watch.]"

—Mark 13:33–37

In the King James Version, verse 34 begins: "For the Son of man is..." This was *mere guesswork* on the part of the translators. The Greek manuscripts make no mention of "the Son of man" here. The translators added the expression because they supposed, without textual evidence, that it *should* have been there.

The manuscripts do have the equivalent of "going on a journey," as well as "and puts his servants in charge, each with his work." These phrases, however, do not fit the original parable. In the first place, if a man went out to a banquet or other social occasion, he would assign a doorkeeper *for the night*. He would not, by contrast, have expected the same man to stay awake twenty-four hours a day while he took a trip for an indefinite period of time. This could take weeks, or even months. Someone added "going on a journey" to the parable, to refer to the time between the resurrection of Jesus and his expected return in glory.

Also, the statement about putting his servants in charge misses the point. The parable's focus is *one* doorkeeper and his

85

alertness, not a whole staff of servants. In the early church, this addition served as a warning to ministers and deacons to carry out their duties faithfully until Jesus returns.

Verse 37 is redundant. To the early church, the addition meant: "This means you, too!" In other words, lay members must also "watch" for the Lord's return.

Waiting for future change thus became, for many people, a substitute for receiving the kingdom of God in the present. What Jesus used to refer to an inner awakening and healing was modified to refer to an expected external event. Reflecting on the trends of modern biblical scholarship, Crossan concludes:

> This constant and increasing loss of the future polarity in the supposed present-future tension of Jesus' teaching has led to the suggestion that Jesus may not have been talking at all in our concept of linear time and that any present and/or future polarity is quite inadequate to his intention.... It is the view of time as man's future that Jesus opposed in the name of time as God's present, not as eternity beyond us but *as advent within us.*[2]

Finally, according to the original Aramaic, the word translated "watch" should instead be rendered "keep awake" or "keep alert."

Based on the above analysis, the original parable would have been approximately as follows:

> Take heed, keep alert. It is like a man when he leaves home and commands the doorkeeper to be on the watch. Keep alert therefore—for you do not know when the master of the house will come, in the evening, or at midnight, or at cockcrow, or in the morning—lest he come suddenly and find you asleep.

The master of the house, then, goes away for the evening. He assigns a man to guard the door while he is gone. His job is to let in people who belong there, and to keep out those who don't.

As the parable is about ourselves, we are both the master and the doorkeeper. The master is the Christ, our spiritual identity. The doorkeeper is our conscious phase of mind. The Christ idea is eternally perfect. The conscious mind, by contrast, is imperfect and in need of instruction.

There *is* a second coming of Christ, but it is a realization of *our own* Christ self. In this consciousness, we find ourselves in a spiritual world governed by spiritual laws. We are not merely vehicles of expression for the truth—we have the truth itself within us. There are thus two points at which we can enter the world of this parable: as the master who returns, or as the doorkeeper who awaits his appearance and opens the door to him.

On the level of the doorkeeper, the conscious phase of mind, we are to be spiritually awake and alert. We allow in thoughts and images that are positive, constructive, and life-giving, and screen out those that are not. As we focus on what is good and true, the Christ consciousness and power are revealed to us inwardly, and this is the master's return. To keep alert, however, requires a high vision and a positive attitude of mind. The other choice is to fall asleep; as in the wheat and the tares, this means to be careless, negative, and indifferent.

Diligence in good and true thoughts is vital. Guard the door of your soul as a sentry, letting only the positive enter. Keep the mental and emotional riff-raff out. Do not even *think* anything evil. As Paul declared in Philippians 4:8:

> Finally, brethren, whatever is true, whatever is honorable, whatever is just, whatever is pure, whatever is lovely, whatever is gracious, if there is any excellence, if there is anything worthy of praise, think about these things.

Affirmations

I am the master, the Christ consciousness that is perfect and eternal.

I am the doorkeeper. I stand guard at the door of my thought.

I am alert to the Christ mind within, and receive its perfect ideas as they are revealed to me.

I receive into my consciousness:
Whatever is true.
Whatever is honorable.
Whatever is just.
Whatever is pure.
Whatever is beautiful.
Whatever is gracious.
Whatever is excellent.
Whatever is worthy of praise.

Chapter 17

The Faithful Servants/Servant Entrusted with Supervision

³⁵"Let your loins be girded and your lamps burning, ³⁶and be like men who are waiting for their master to come home from the marriage feast, so that they may open to him at once when he comes and knocks. ³⁷Blessed are those servants whom the master finds awake when he comes; truly, I say to you, he will gird himself and have them sit at table, and he will come and serve them. ³⁸If he comes in the second watch, or in the third, and finds them so, blessed are those servants! [³⁹But know this, that if the householder had known at what hour the thief was coming, he would have been awake and would not have left his house to be broken into. {⁴⁰You also must be ready; for the Son of man is coming at an hour you do not expect.}"

⁴¹Peter said, "Lord, are you telling this parable for us or for all?"] ⁴²And the Lord said, "Who then is the faithful and wise steward, whom his master will set over his household, to give them their portion of food at the proper time? ⁴³Blessed is that servant whom his master when he comes will find so doing. ⁴⁴Truly I tell you, he will set him over all his possessions. ⁴⁵But if that servant says to himself, 'My master is delayed in coming,' and begins to beat the menservants and the maidservants, and to eat and drink and get drunk, ⁴⁶the master of that servant will come on a day when he does not expect him and at an hour he does not know, and will punish him, and put him with the unfaithful. [⁴⁷And that servant who knew his master's will, but did not make ready or act according to his will, shall receive a severe beating. ⁴⁸But he who did not know, and did what deserved a beating, shall receive a light beating. Every one to whom much is given, of him will much be

**required; and of him to whom men commit much they will
demand the more.]"**
                —Luke 12:35–48 (partial parallel: Matthew 24:42–51)

This section continues the master-servant theme. It
enlarges upon the rewards of faithful service, as well as the
penalties for failing that trust. The text is a composite from a
literary point of view. There is not just one parable here, but
two—or three, if the simile of the burglar be counted. Its com-
ponent parts are as follows:

12:35-38—The Faithful Servants (no parallel)
12:39—The Burglar (parallels: Matthew 24:43; Thomas 21,103)
12:40—Interpretation of the Burglar (parallel: Matthew 24:44)
12:41—Peter's Question (no parallel)
12:42-46—The Servant Entrusted with Supervision (parallel:
      Matthew 24:45-51)
12:47-48a—Degrees of Punishment (no parallel)
12:48b—An Independent Saying (no parallel)

The Faithful Servants (12:35–38)

The parables in 12:35–38 and 12:42–46 did not originally
belong together. Despite the question in 12:42—"Who then is
the faithful and wise steward?"—the second parable does not
really explain the first, "Blessed are those servants whom the
master finds awake.... " For another, the partial parallel in
Matthew 24:45-51—"Who then is the faithful and wise servant
...?"—claims no connection with the parable of the faithful servants. That is to say, Matthew is apparently giving us an interpretation, without including a text to be interpreted. The obvious
conclusion is that Matthew 24:45-51/Luke 12:42-46 is an independent parable, not a mere commentary on Luke 12:35-38.

Girding the loins, mentioned in Luke 12:35, meant prepar-
ing for hard or serious work. A workman would tuck the end of
his robe into a kind of girdle, so that it would not become dirty
or interfere with his work.[3] The burning lamp again may be
understood as an illumined state of consciousness. "Let your

loins be girded and your lamps burning" thus advises: Work to keep your thinking positive, and be attuned to the inner light.

In the old Near Eastern culture, a man attending a feast paid no heed to coming or going "on time." He might return home at any hour. If he could afford hired servants, they had to stay up until his return. This required effort and self-discipline on their part, but they would be rewarded in some way by a grateful master.

According to the parable, the master "will gird himself and have them sit at table, and he will come and serve them." This could be typical Near Eastern exaggerated expression, but nevertheless it points to Jesus' central meaning: If we serve the Christ mind, we shall in turn be served by it. If we humble ourselves to the formative power of thought, using it in positive ways, it will exalt us with positive results. It is a matter of cause and effect, of action and reaction.

The Burglar and Its Interpretation (12:39–40)

The comparison of the coming of the master with the breaking in of a burglar is difficult to interpret without knowing its original context. Jesus probably didn't intend that the thief be used as a symbol of the kingdom of God. We remember his words in John 10:10, "The thief comes only to steal and kill and destroy; I came that they may have life, and have it abundantly." Also, while the burglar (in Luke 12:39 and Matthew 24:43) is connected with the appearance of "the Son of man," this is not true for the versions in Thomas 21 and 103. For these reasons, we should disregard Luke 12:40–"You also must be ready; for the Son of man is coming at an hour you do not expect"–and Matthew 24:44 as later additions.

It is interesting to contrast this parable concerning watching against burglars, with the familiar words of Matthew 6:19, which declare:

> Do not lay up for yourselves treasures on earth, where moth
> and rust consume and where thieves break in and steal.

These words suggest that we should not amass such riches that we find ourselves embroiled in the problems of protecting our goods from thievery. On the other hand, we have recently come upon the words from Thomas 21 which go back to the matter of protecting our goods.

> Therefore I say to you, if the owner of a house knows that the thief is coming, he will begin his vigil before he comes and will not let him dig through into his house of his domain to carry away his goods.

> You, then, be on your guard against the world. Arm yourselves with great strength lest the robbers find a way to come to you, for the difficulty which you expect will surely materialize.

It is possible, though by no means certain, that this reading is original. Inasmuch as our supreme sense of worth comes from the recognition of "God within," then it is our business to keep up our guard against those about us who by deriding remarks and sneering comments would destroy this sense of ultimate value. The parable viewed not from a simple material standpoint, but rather from the higher plane of spiritual and moral values, makes sense.

Playing over and over again in our minds negative thoughts will surely attract more. As the version in Thomas 21 says, "The difficulty which you expect will surely materialize." The same thought had been said long before in the words of Job 3:25:

> The thing that I fear comes upon me,
> and what I dread befalls me.

Peter's Question (12:41) "Lord, are you telling this parable for us or for all?"

This verse serves as a transition between the parables. It is not authentic, but a mere literary device. In fact, the parable that follows does not really answer the question posed as to whether Luke 12:35–38 applies only to the inner circle, or to everyone. Also, the parallel passage in Matthew 24:42–51 omits this question.

The Servant Entrusted with Supervision (12:42–46)

Every person is a steward. We are entrusted with the supervision of our thoughts and words. We are set over the household of our soul, which, in a larger sense, is not our own but the temple of God. If we feed our consciousness with divine ideas of life, love, and truth we are, in the parable's terms, giving our thoughts "their portion of food at the proper time." This is what "the faithful and wise steward" does. By obeying his master's will, he received dominion. "He will set him over all his possessions."

The ability to choose, however, includes the capacity to make wrong choices. To beat the menservants is to entertain negative *thoughts*. To beat the maidservants is to indulge in negative *emotions* such as hate, fear, envy, and greed. Getting drunk is an ancient symbol of spiritual ignorance.[4] Verse 46 warns us that the creative law cannot be misused with impunity. If the steward in the parable is unfaithful, he will be punished.

Degrees of Punishment (12:47–48a)

The parallel passage in Matthew 24:42–51 makes no mention of this section. What is more, 12:47–48a, "And that servant who knew his master's will ..." does not fit the context of 12:42–46, "Who then is the faithful and wise steward ...?" The parable in 12:42–46 is about a steward—*one person*—who *knew* the nature of his duties. He had to choose how he would run his master's household. In fact, Jesus left it to his hearers to speculate on whether this steward would be faithful or not. By contrast, 12:47–48a (i.e. ending with the words, "light beating") mentions *two servants*. One knew his duty, but the other did not know. The willful offender gets a more severe beating than the fool who didn't know better. For these reasons, the "degrees of punishment" section must be a later addition.

An Independent Saying (12:48b)

> Everyone to whom much is given, of him will much be
>   required; and of him to whom men commit much
>   they will demand the more.

Although secondary to the context, this is an authentic say-ing of Jesus. To whom much is given, much is required. That is to say, the more we are illumined in spiritual truth, the greater our calling to share that understanding with others. We cannot continue our inner awakening unless we express and radiate the love, the joy, and the peace that we have already received. A fountain, in order to receive more water, must give out the water that it already has. The choice we have is like the differ-ence between a clean and free-flowing fountain, and the stench of stagnant waters.

Affirmations

I am alive, alert, and awake to the indwelling Christ.

I am inspired by divine ideas at all times.

My soul and body are the temple of the Holy Spirit.

I honor this shrine of the Spirit with positive thoughts, images, words, and actions.

Chapter 18

The Talents

[14]"For it will be as when a man going on a journey called his servants and entrusted to them his property; [15]to one he gave five talents, to another two, to another one, to each according to his ability. Then he went away. [16]He who had received the five talents went at once and traded with them; and he made five talents more. [17]So also, he who had the two talents made two talents more. [18]But he who had received the one talent went and dug in the ground and hid his master's money. [19]Now after a long time the master of those servants came and settled accounts with them. [20]And he who had received the five talents came forward, bringing five talents more, saying, 'Master, you delivered to me five talents; here I have made five talents more.' [21]His master said to him, 'Well done, good and faithful servant; you have been faithful over a little, I will set you over much; enter into the joy of your master.' [22]And he also who had the two talents came forward, saying, 'Master, you delivered to me two talents; here I have made two talents more.' [23]His master said to him, 'Well done, good and faithful servant; you have been faithful over a little, I will set you over much; enter into the joy of your master.' [24]He also who had received the one talent came forward, saying, 'Master, I knew you to be a hard man, reaping where you did not sow, and gathering where you did not winnow; [25]so I was afraid, and I went and hid your talent in the ground. Here you have what is yours.' [26]But his master answered him, 'You wicked and slothful servant! You knew that I reap where I have not sowed, and gather where I have not winnowed? [27]Then you ought to have invested my money with the bankers, and at my coming I should have received what was my own with interest. [28]So take the talent from him,

and give it to him who has the ten talents. [29]For to every one who has will more be given, and he will have abundance; but from him who has not, even what he has will be taken away. [[30]And cast the worthless servant into the outer darkness; there men will weep and gnash their teeth.]' "

—Matthew 25:14-30 (parallel passage: Luke 19:12-27)

The talent was a large monetary unit. Estimates differ as to how much one was worth. The issue is complicated by the fact that there were gold talents and silver ones. Then as now, gold carried many times more value than silver. According to a footnote in the Revised Standard Version (New Testament dating from 1946), the talent was probably worth about $1,000. This figure must be adjusted upward because of inflation.

Luke 19:12-27, a somewhat similar text, is called the parable of the pounds, based on the translation of the ancient *mina* into the British pound sterling in the King James and other versions. Scholars debate as to whether the two parables go back to one parable, or to two. In either case, it is likely that the authors of Matthew and Luke, respectively, drew upon versions that were already quite different.

The version in Matthew, as it now stands, is more original than the one in Luke. Luke 19:12-27 reflects an attempt to merge an independent parable with that of the pounds. This parable—of which Matthew 25:14-30 bears no trace—is about a claimant to a throne who goes away to receive kingly power, and later returns. It is the subject of Chapter 27, "The Throne Claimant."

Matthew 25:13, which precedes the text we are using, reads: "Watch, therefore, for you know neither the day nor the hour." This places the parable in an erroneous context. For the story's theme is not about a future Second Coming, but how we might think and act in the present. Also, the ending in verse 30 is out of context. In the first place, Luke's version lacks this statement. Second, the servant with one talent had lost his money. There is no point to adding a second punishment, i.e. to throw him "into the outer darkness" as well.

Verse 29 reads: "For to every one who has will more be

given, and he will have abundance; but from him who has not, even what he has will be taken away." This was a "floating" saying that also appears in Matthew 13:12, Mark 4:25, Luke 8:18, and Thomas 41. Nevertheless its connection with the parable is probably original. As already noted, the authors of Matthew and Luke very likely drew upon separate sources for the two versions of this parable. Yet, despite wide differences on other points, the parable of the pounds includes a similar wording in Luke 19:26. The agreement of Matthew 25:29 and Luke 19:26 thus strongly indicates that Jesus himself used this saying to conclude the original parable.

In addition, Matthew 25:29, "to every one who has will more be given," fits the parable's teaching. It is a way of saying that like attracts like, and like produces like. Thoughts and attitudes based on abundance and success attract and produce more abundance and success. Thoughts and attitudes based on poverty and lack will attract and produce more poverty and lack. This does not mean that we cannot change the direction of our thinking. We *can* change, and Jesus' parables give us the essential keys for doing so.

In Matthew's text, we find that the first man used five talents and made five more. The second used two, and made two more. The third buried his one talent, and lost even that to the man with the ten talents.

A basic principle of this parable, then, is that *use is the law of increase*. Investing money wisely is here a symbol of investing thought, time, and energy in any positive activity. A painter's skill, the power of a muscle, and the fruits of constructive thinking all increase by the same law. Though the double meaning of "talent" is a coincidence, this parable applies to developing our God-given talents, so that we may increase our skill and effectiveness. And this point, though it will appear trite to some readers, is no small matter.

In verse 19, the master returns home and settles accounts with his servants. This is in the form of *reward and punishment*. The meaning to which it points, however, is *cause and effect, whether positive or negative*. It is as much a symbol of creative law as planting seeds in the ground and reaping the harvest that follows.

To his two faithful servants, he said: "You have been faithful over a little, I will set you over much; enter into the joy of your master" (25:21,23). By contrast, the servant with one talent was afraid, and buried it. Because of his refusal to act, to step out in faith, and to take a risk, he lost even what he had. It has been said that "your greatest mistake is your fear of making one." Again, God blesses us with certain abilities and potentials. We are to develop and use them to the fullest, and then trust God to bless us and supply our needs.

The first and second servants trusted the integrity of their employer, who cheerfully rewarded them for their honest efforts. The third servant viewed his master as a hard man, who reaped where he did not sow, and gathered where he did not winnow. Only the third man lost out, for his master acted toward him exactly as he expected. In a similar sense, people, animals, things, and the earth itself bend to fit the images and expectations that we hold in mind.

The third servant says, in effect: "The responsibility rests on you, the boss, not on me." He believed himself to be a victim of circumstance, and projected his feelings upon his boss. This, however, was a misperception. No one is a victim unless he thinks and believes that he is. In the kingdom of God, everyone is one with God and therefore sovereign; there are no victims and no victimizers.

In summary, then, if we fail to be responsible in thought and action, and view ourselves as victims, we shall, for all intents and purposes, become victims. If, on the other hand, we do the best we can in thought, word, and action, and trust the spiritual universe to create a just return, we shall grow, progress, and prosper.

Affirmations

With the cosmic Christ at the center of my being, I am a victor in life, not a victim.

I accept and apply the fact that use is the law of increase.

I accept and apply the fact that practice makes perfect.

I use every positive thought and word to the greatest extent possible.

I reject every negative thought and word as unreal and powerless.

I apply myself in positive actions to the greatest extent possible.

I reject every negative action and habit as unreal and powerless.

Having done all, I relax, let go, and let God.

Chapter 19

The Laborers in the Vineyard

[1]"For the kingdom of heaven is like a householder who went out early in the morning to hire laborers for his vineyard. [2]After agreeing with the laborers for a denarius a day, he sent them into his vineyard. [3]And going about the third hour he saw others standing idle in the market place; [4]and to them he said, 'You go into the vineyard too, and whatever is right I will give you.' So they went. [5]Going out again about the sixth hour and the ninth hour, he did the same. [6]And about the eleventh hour he went out and found others standing; and he said to them, 'Why do you stand here idle all day?' [7]They said to him, 'Because no one has hired us.' He said to them, 'You go into the vineyard too.' [8]And when evening came, the owner of the vineyard said to his steward, 'Call the laborers and pay them their wages, beginning with the last, up to the first.' [9]And when those hired about the eleventh hour came, each of them received a denarius. [10]Now when the first came, they thought they would receive more; but each of them also received a denarius. [11]And on receiving it they grumbled at the householder, [12]saying, 'These last worked only one hour, and you have made them equal to us who have borne the burden of the day and the scorching heat.' [13]But he replied to one of them, 'Friend, I am doing you no wrong; did you not agree with me for a denarius? [[14]Take what belongs to you, and go; I choose to give to this last as I give to you. [15]Am I not allowed to do what I choose with what belongs to me? Or do you begrudge my generosity?' [16]So the last will be first, and the first last.]"   —*Matthew 20:1–16*

According to tradition, this parable's central purpose is to teach the grace of God. Readers note that all the workers receive the same pay, no matter how long or how short the period in which they worked in the vineyard. The payment of the same wages for unequal work upsets our human concept of fairness. This would create a serious problem if applied to labor-management relations. It is deemed acceptable, however, when applied to the manner in which God receives a repentant soul.

This parable relates to the fact that the grace of God, when received into our consciousness, progressively cancels the results of our past negative thoughts and actions. No matter how valid the teaching, however, it is doubtful that Jesus intended *this* parable as an image of the prevalence of grace over karma. The central problem is that the denarius was a bare subsistence wage. If Jesus had designed the parable for this purpose, the householder would have paid all the workmen more generously.

The following facts should be noted: The King James Version, first published in 1611, translates the denarius as a penny. An old nursery rhyme, dating from roughly the same period, tells that bakers sold hot-cross buns in two sizes, one for 1¢ and two for 1¢. With the progress of inflation, the Revised Standard Version (1946) states that "The denarius was worth about 20¢." Today this would be close to a full dollar. Even when allowing for the fact that money goes further in some parts of the Near East, a dollar a day is by any estimate a minimum wage.

It is the nature of our Father-Mother God to give lavishly of every benefit. Divine grace is not penurious. The infinite mind does not reduce people to what Douglas MacArthur called "a universal level of mediocrity." As Ephesians 3:20 declares, "The power at work within us is able to do far more abundantly than all that we ask or think." Again, we read in John 1:16: "From his fullness have we all received, grace upon grace."

Also, it is likely that this parable originally ended with the question, "Friend, I am doing you no wrong; did you not agree with me for a denarius?" (20:13). John Dominic Crossan gives sound reasons for this conclusion.[5] He notes, for example, that it is not at all obvious that the householder's action is good or generous as he claims in 20:15. It would have been better had he paid all the workers a denarius an hour.

Note especially that 20:13 refers again to the terms under which the laborers had accepted employment in 20:2. They had had *a meeting of the minds* with their employer, to the effect that the pay for the day's work would be one denarius. This settles the issue, making the statements following in 20:14–15 superfluous.

Jesus' analogies about vines and vineyards point to our own inner life, meaning our consciousness and what we choose to do with it. We are all workers in the vineyard of the mind, and his vineyard imagery points to different aspects of the subject. Some scholars look for a wider Mediterranean or Near Eastern context for grape imagery, and this is valid.[6] However, in so doing we should not overlook the Old Testament prophets. Philip J. King, referring to the book of Hosea, writes in part:

> Grape-growing is a rich source of imagery in the Bible, especially with the eighth-century prophets. The vine symbolizes peace, prosperity, and fertility. The vine was also a national symbol, as Hosea indicates: "Israel is a luxuriant vine that yields its fruit" (Hosea 10:1).[7]

The specific parable we are considering depicts one element of mental cause and effect, which is the "fertile ground" of our everyday lives. The householder pays the workers according to the agreement they made with him. In like manner, a person is compensated according to the "agreement" he makes with life. We can call it a "meeting of the minds" between the individual and the creative law.

The work of trimming vines in the hot, subtropical sun becomes increasingly tedious as the temperature rises, sunburn becomes a problem, and hands become worn and sore. It has been compared in these respects to picking cotton in the American south, where "cotton-picking" is a metaphor for anything unpleasant. In this parable, Jesus challenged his hearers to question their own false sense of weakness, poverty, and lack. They had thought in too small terms of themselves and of the scope of their lives. God has no limits; as his infinite idea, neither do we. Divine Mind has given us everything, through the indwelling Christ. Yet people tend to become trapped in their self-made concepts of limitation, and because of this they suffer.

God's plan for each of our lives is far greater, happier, and more fulfilling than anything we could plan for ourselves. The acceptance of this plan is the way to health, success, and abundance. We need not bargain for the husks of life when we are heirs to the whole estate.

Jessie B. Rittenhouse captured the essence of our parable in a poem:

> I bargained with Life for a penny,
> And Life would pay no more,
> However I begged at evening
> When I counted my scanty store.
> For Life is a just employer;
> He gives you what you ask,
> But once you have set the wages,
> Why, you must bear the task.
> I worked for a menial's hire,
> Only to learn, dismayed,
> That any wage I had asked of Life,
> Life would have paid.[8]

Affirmations

I cancel all claims of limitation that I have made.

I am open to life in all its fullness. God is life, and he gives me the fullness of life.

I work with God in all that I think, say, and do.

As I accept God's plan for my life, and work with the plan, I am abundantly prospered.

Chapter 20

The Unprofitable Servant

> ⁷"Will any one of you, who has a servant plowing or keeping sheep, say to him when he has come in from the field, 'Come at once and sit down at table'? ⁸Will he not rather say to him, 'Prepare supper for me, and gird yourself and serve me, till I eat and drink; and afterward you shall eat and drink'? ⁹Does he thank the servant because he did what was commanded? ¹⁰So you also, when you have done all that is commanded you, say, 'We are unworthy servants; we have only done what was our duty.' "
>
> *—Luke 17:7–10*

This parable is unusual, in the way that Jesus called upon his listeners to respond. They would have answered aloud to his three questions. Verses 7, 8, and 9, respectively, call for answers of No–Yes–No. Then in verse 10, he tells them to be like loyal and humble servants who keep working hard without complaint.

If the servant in the parable seems to have a hard lot in life, let us consider the context of the times. Laborers did not punch a time clock in biblical days. There were no unions, and no collective bargaining. In the modern western world, most employees work a given number of hours and then spend the rest of them as they choose. In the traditional Orient, it was not so. They were expected to keep busy every waking hour, and to remain on call at all times.

George Lamsa, speaking of those ancient conditions which still prevailed in his youth, explained:

Eastern servants never complain of their hard labors and long hours. Instead, they always tell their lord that there

104

isn't enough work to be done and that they are idle. If they say otherwise they would be branded as lazy and no one would hire them. When a servant tells his master that he is idle for lack of work, his lord trusts him more and gives him privileges. But those servants who complain are assigned to harder tasks and are liable to be discharged.[9]

Applied on a mental and spiritual level, which is Jesus' real intent, the parable tells us to persist in meditation and constructive thinking. We are to keep on, without becoming lax or forgetting the true basis of thought in the omnipresence of God. That is to say, our spiritual vision needs to be honored and applied continually, and in all situations. The more we think the truth for its own sake, rather than for its rewards, the more benefits we will release into our everyday lives. As we serve the Christ, our basic spiritual identity, we gradually become awakened to our own mastery.

Luke 17:5-6, which precedes this parable, reads:

The apostles said to the Lord, "Increase our faith!" And the Lord said, "If you had faith as a grain of mustard seed, you could say to this sycamine tree, 'Be rooted up, and be planted in the sea,' and it would obey you."

While many settings claimed for the parables are doubtful, this one may well be original. According to the context in Luke, the apostles asked Jesus to increase their faith. He replied by making two statements: In 17:5-6, he dramatically expressed the power of a quickened faith. He did not mean that a little faith will accomplish great things, but that quickened faith has a tremendous power of increase. This again is the message of the mustard seed.

In his second statement (17:7-10), he qualified the previous one by saying, in effect, "You will have to work continually on releasing your faith."

Jesus could not, of course, *give* them faith. They already had this faculty inherent within them, as we have it in ourselves. What he did, with consummate skill, was to bring balance into the discussion. A quickened faith is an act of God's grace, but its practical application still requires constant practice. The unlimited power of God is already within, but we have to work with it faithfully in order to express it.

Affirmations

I am ready to put aside all errors. I am ready to receive the power of a quickened faith.

I serve the law of my being, the Christ. I attune to all that is positive in thought, word, and action.

The mind of Christ increases within me. Its power is released in mind, body, and affairs.

Chapter 21

The Unrighteous Steward

¹He also said to the disciples, "There was a rich man who had a steward, and charges were brought to him that this man was wasting his goods. ²And he called him and said to him, 'What is this that I hear about you? Turn in the account of your stewardship, for you can no longer be steward.' ³And the steward said to himself, 'What shall I do, since my master is taking the stewardship away from me? I am not strong enough to dig, and I am ashamed to beg. ⁴I have decided what to do, so that people may receive me into their houses when I am put out of the stewardship.' ⁵So, summoning his master's debtors one by one, he said to the first, 'How much do you owe my master?' ⁶He said, 'A hundred measures of oil.' And he said to him, 'Take your bill, and sit down quickly and write fifty.' ⁷Then he said to another, 'And how much do you owe?' He said, 'A hundred measures of wheat.' He said to him, 'Take your bill, and write eighty.' ⁸The master commended the dishonest steward for his prudence; for the sons of this world are wiser in their own generation than the sons of light. [⁹And I tell you, make friends for yourselves by means of unrighteous mammon, so that when it fails they may receive you into the eternal habitations. ¹⁰He who is faithful in a very little is faithful also in much; and he who is dishonest in a very little is dishonest also in much. ¹¹If then you have not been faithful in the unrighteous mammon, who will entrust to you the true riches? ¹²And if you have not been faithful in that which is another's, who will give you that which is your own? ¹³No servant can serve two masters; for either he will hate the one and love the other, or he will be devoted to the one and despise the other. You cannot serve God and mammon.]"

–Luke 16:1–13

Many readers find this a difficult parable. Why, people ask, did the rich man give his dishonest steward a compliment after he falsified his business records? The parables of the laborers in the vineyard (Matthew 20:1–13) and the unprofitable servant (Luke 17:7–10) reflect labor practices that are unacceptable by modern standards. Here, however, the actions of the steward are worse because they are willfully and deliberately dishonest.

Some say that the message is simply a matter of taking bold and decisive action when a situation requires it. Our parable, taken as a whole, does not appear to be designed for only that purpose. It also does not resolve the ethical issue which tends to distract from, rather than to illustrate, such a meaning.

First century Christians also found this parable difficult as they tried to get a handle on its real message. A detailed review of Luke 16:8–13 reveals four distinct interpretations, i.e. as found in verses 8, 9, 10–12, and 13. The simile of the two masters (verse 13) seems out of context, since it also appears in Matthew 6:24 and Thomas 47. This raises a question as to the context of all four commentaries.

Parables scholars differ as to where Jesus ended his discourse. Opinions include:

(1) At the end of 16:7.

(2) With 16:8a: "The master commended the dishonest steward for his prudence."

(3) At the end of 16:8.

While this issue may never be solved conclusively, opinion 3 is more likely to be correct. Verse 8 can be read as an exaggerated expression followed by a proverb: "The master commended the dishonest steward for his prudence; for the sons of this world are wiser in their own generation than the sons of light." Taken by itself, the master's praise (16:8a) would amount to an endorsement of dishonesty. By retaining the complete verse—including the polarity between "the sons of this world" and "the sons of light"—Jesus' true intention can in all likelihood be found.

Let us briefly review the cultural background. In biblical times, a steward had an honored position. A rich man would give his trusted steward pretty much of a free hand. He received no salary, but had ready access to his master's money. He made important business decisions as well as handling the household expenses.

The steward's accusers in the parable would have been hired servants of a lower status. Being jealous, they would have not only complained to their employer, but also spread damaging gossip. In the parable, the rich man believed the accusations and told the steward to turn in his business records, for he was to be fired.

The steward, faced with a hard decision, resolved to take swift and decisive action. He called in his employer's debtors, and falsified the books to reduce their debts. A man who owed one hundred measures of oil had his liability reduced to fifty. Another debtor, who owed one hundred measures of wheat, had the figure reduced to eighty. The steward did this in the hope that one of them would make him steward, or at least give him some sort of job.

Students of ethics debate as to *the degree of fault* in the steward's actions. Looking at ethical standards as absolute, there is of course no excuse for his actions. Viewing such standards as relative, however, and considering his possible family obligations, one would take a more tolerant view. According to George Lamsa—who wrote from first-hand experience—the traditional Near Eastern society is dominated by bribery and corruption, and friendships are openly bought and sold.[10]

Crossan has correctly observed that sometimes Jesus used parables to shock his listeners. Such would have been the effect of "for the sons of this world are wiser in their own generation than the sons of light"(16:8b). Such words would be shocking to Pharisees and any others who considered themselves more righteous than the common people about them.

Another possible view is to examine the deeper, often hidden meaning of the imagery which Jesus used. Jesus spoke of leaven as an image of the activity of spiritual consciousness in the soul; as in Matthew 13:33: "The kingdom of heaven is like leaven which a woman took and hid in three measures of meal, till it was all leavened." This passage, which is also found in

Luke 13:20-21 and Thomas 96, sees the leaven of the kingdom of God in the individual soul as a healing, vitalizing symbol. To the chaotic, fragmented consciousness of error, however, this inner activity is corrupting and destructive. From the standpoint of the kingdom, the reduction of debts in the parable is analogous to spiritual consciousness decreasing karmic debts. This is a victory for grace, which transcends the law of relative cause and effect and produces forgiveness. It is dishonest and corrupting, however, from the viewpoint of strict justice, which requires punishment for every false belief and negative action of the past.

The more probable interpretation, however—without disallowing others—includes 16:8 and treats it as a key passage. The sons "of this world," in Greek *tou aionōs*, would be more correctly translated "of this age." *Aiōn* refers to world in a temporal sense, unlike *kosmos* which makes reference to world in a spatial sense. Our text means persons of a certain era or time cycle, who represent *a particular belief system*. There is also an implied contrast between the ways and conditions of a given time and society, and ways and conditions of the new era which is sure to come.

"Sons of light" is an Essene expression. According to the Dead Sea Scrolls, the sons of light (or children of light) are the enlightened Essenes. Jesus used the term in a wider sense to mean *all those who are illumined through the inner light*. "While you have the light, believe in the light, that you may become sons of light" (John 12:36). We thus have a contrast between two mind-sets or ways of viewing reality, which lead to different ways of ordering one's life and affairs.

The text asserts that in some important sense, the unworldly can take a lesson from the worldly wise. A vital need, then, is to discern the sense in which the "sons of this world" tend to be wiser or more prudent than the "sons of light." This is not mysterious or difficult. Worldly people (of either sex) sometimes adhere to their standards with greater fidelity and skill than the unworldly do to theirs. The steward may have been consistently wrong, but at least he was consistent. He faithfully followed his sense of what is expedient. Here, then, is the point: consistency is what the children of light need in applying *their own* standards, *their own* vision of reality. The parables as a whole give us the vision of a spiritual universe, governed by spiritual laws. We can, if we choose, accept their frame of reference, make it our own, and apply it to our everyday lives.

The steward's authority over his master's money and goods compares with our access to divine ideas and resources. We are all stewards in the realm of divine Mind. The children of light need to take a step beyond being illumined from within. They need to make the omnipresence of God not an escape from "the world," but a frame of reference to guide them at all times. The realization that God is the only presence and only mind is to be taken to its logical conclusion in thought, word, and action. Then, and then only, can its transforming power be fully released in and through us.

Affirmations

I am freed from the bondage of worldly thought.

I am ushered into the new era of liberty and light.

I accept the omnipresence without reserve. I am resolved to see in every place, time, and condition only the one presence and one power.

I believe in the presence of good only, and look for the good always.

I am the perfect manifestation of a perfect God.

Chapter 22

The Wicked Husbandmen/
Rejected Cornerstone

[65]He said, "There was a good man who owned a vineyard. He leased it to tenant farmers so that they might work it and he might collect the produce from them. He sent his servant so that the tenants might give him the produce of the vineyard. They seized his servant and beat him, all but killing him. The servant went back and told his master. The master said, 'Perhaps he did not recognize them.' He sent another servant. The tenants beat this one as well. Then the owner sent his son and said, 'Perhaps they will show respect to my son.' Because the tenants knew that it was he who was the heir to the vineyard, they seized him and killed him. [Let him who has ears hear.]"
[66]Jesus said, "Show me the stone which the builders have rejected. That one is the cornerstone."
—Thomas 65–66 (parallel passages: Matthew 21:33–46; Mark 12:1–12; Luke 20:9–19)

Tracing the various threads within this parable becomes a fascinating exercise as we seek to lift the basic truth from the lips of Jesus. A problem with the text becomes apparent when we compare the four widely different versions of this parable. Those in the gospels of Mark and Thomas appear to have been transmitted separately, probably first by word of mouth and later in written form. The versions in Matthew and Luke, however, are related to that in Mark. As both Mark 12:1 and Matthew 21:33 mention a hedge, a winepress, and a tower, Matthew's dependence on Mark is here certain. The absence of these images in Luke makes it likely that Luke drew not from the biblical Mark, but from a major source-document of Mark that made no mention of a hedge, winepress, or tower. Since Thomas also omits all three, it is unlikely that they were part of the original parable.

The basic meaning that Jesus had in mind for this parable rests largely with the question: "What did he intend by the vineyard?" It is in the vineyard that the tenants usurp the owner's authority. It is here that they defy and beat his servants, and kill his son and heir.

Church tradition relates the vineyard to Israel. The context, as given in Matthew, Mark, and Luke, supports this conclusion. According to this view, the tenants are the Jewish ecclesiastical leaders. The servants who are beaten, stoned, and killed are the prophets who received such treatment. In Mark 12:4, the single servant whom "they wounded...in the head" is probably John the Baptist. Finally, the son and heir is Jesus. In Mark 12:8, the wicked tenants "took him and killed him, and cast him out of the vineyard [Israel]." Matthew 21:39 revised this to read "they took him and cast him out of the vineyard [here Jerusalem], and killed him."

Both Matthew 21:33 and Mark 12:1 refer to Isaiah 5:1-2, which uses a vineyard as a symbol of Israel:

> Let me sing for my beloved
> a love song concerning his vineyard:
> My beloved had a vineyard
> on a very fertile hill.
> He digged it and cleared it of stones,
> and planted it with choice vines;
> he built a watchtower in the midst of it,
> and hewed out a wine vat in it;
> and he looked for it to yield grapes,
> but it yielded wild grapes.

The connection, in this parable, between the vineyard and Israel is open to question partly for linguistic reasons: Jesus gave his parables in his native tongue, *Aramaic*. Matthew 21:33 and Mark 12:1, however, draw from the Greek translation of Isaiah, i.e. the *Septuagint*. This is obvious because whereas the Greek text of Isaiah 5:1-2 mentions the hedge found in

Matthew and Mark, the Hebrew text—on which the above translation of this passage is based—does not. It is virtually certain
that Jesus would not have mixed the two completely dissimilar
languages (i.e. Aramaic and Greek) in a given parable. This further strengthens the likelihood that the references in Mark and
Matthew to Isaiah 5:1-2 are a later addition.

Moreover, the differences in the versions in Matthew,
Mark, and Luke show that each editor took rather wide liberties
with the text. Each, within a certain range, did his own thing.
This is in direct contrast to the text in Thomas, which is
remarkably balanced, concise, and consistent.

Matthew, Mark, and Luke state that after the death of his
son, the owner will destroy the false tenants and give the vineyard to others. From the editors' point of view, this meant that
the Jerusalem authorities would be eliminated, and replaced by
Christian leaders in the church. Crossan questions this traditional view on the basis of literary analysis. He wonders, for
example, why the owner would change his actions so abruptly,
and then, after such severe difficulties, rent out the vineyard to
new tenants.[11]

Thomas has no parallel to this, but adds the floating
proverb, "Let him who has ears hear." Without some additional
statement, the parable in Thomas would read like an article
from a scandal sheet. It would be of interest to some readers,
but not edifying in any sense.

In two respects, however, all four sources agree. First, all
four express the theme of *the son's inheritance* in much the
same form. Its status as part of the original parable is thus certain. Second, all our accounts quote Psalm 118:22 as part of
their conclusion: "The stone which the builders rejected has
become the head of the corner." Since both Mark and Thomas
record independent traditions for this parable, it is certain that
Jesus used Psalm 118:22 in this context. Here, then, is the
"additional statement" that the interpreter must consider.
Incidentally, this does not apply to Psalm 118:23, which both
Luke and Thomas omit: "This is the Lord's doing; it is marvelous in our eyes."

Source Document	Wicked Husbandmen	Rejected Cornerstone
OT Book of Psalms	———	118:22–23
Matthew	21:33–41	21:42
Mark	12:1–9	12:10–11
Luke	20:9–16	20:17
Thomas	Saying 65	Saying 66

This careful, literary analysis shows the linkage between the vineyard and Israel to be erroneous. At the same time, it supports the authenticity of the parable itself. It verifies that the original core was close to the shorter form preserved in the gospel of Thomas.

We have already noted, in connection with the laborers in the vineyard (Matthew 20:1–13), that Jesus applied vineyard imagery to our own consciousness and what we do with it. This is also the case here. The vineyard and its fruits do not represent any ecclesiastical group. They point, rather, to the psyche and its potential for positive as well as negative results.

During the first century, most of the arable land in Galilee was held in large estates. In many cases, the owners preferred city life, and only occasionally visited their land and the people who worked it. Traditionally, and even in many countries today, people viewed a landed aristocracy as a source of oppression for good, hard-working tenant farmers.[12] In Thomas, Jesus contrasts a *good* landowner and *wicked* tenants. This seems a deliberate reversal of popular assumptions—a tactic, as Crossan points out, which Jesus used on various occasions. This does not mean that Jesus condoned oppression of the common people. He sought, rather, to overthrow the whole concept of victims vs. victimizers. For in the kingdom of God, everyone is made in the image of God, and all are heirs to all that is in God. Reality is one, and is not in conflict with itself.

To be specific, then, the "good man who owned a vineyard" is every person. The vineyard is the mind, the cultivated area of consciousness which each of us must tend. The wicked tenants are negative beliefs, habits, and attitudes that have usurped the soul. The servants are divine ideas that the ego rejects. The tenants' final act of defiance, in killing the son,

refers to the rejection of the soul's true heir, the indwelling
Christ.

Thomas 65 leaves the vineyard in the hands of the rebels.
Psalm 118:22, quoted by Thomas 66, shifts metaphors, giving
the cornerstone as the solution. The significance of this is as follows: The son's inheritance includes all the infinite ideas that
inhere in the mind of Christ. The I AM or Christ self "comes,"
in a psychological sense, to replace the false beliefs, habits, and
attitudes which the wicked tenants represent. The stone, our
true spiritual identity, becomes the head of the corner, the
foundation of all thought. So in this metaphoric sense the
wicked tenants *are* cast out; what is implicit in Thomas is made
explicit in Matthew, Mark, and Luke.

Isaiah 28:16 declares:

> Therefore thus says the Lord God, "Behold, I am laying in
> Zion for a foundation a stone, a tested stone, a precious
> cornerstone, of a sure foundation."

The New Testament also refers to the "stone" theme in
other contexts. For example:

> Come to him, to that living stone, rejected by men but in
> God's sight chosen and precious; and like living stones be
> yourselves built into a spiritual house [consciousness].
> —1 Peter 2:4–5

Revelation 2:17 presents the white stone as inwardly contacted and realized:

> He who has an ear, let him hear what the Spirit says to the
> churches. To him who conquers I will give some of the hid-
> den manna, and I will give him a white stone, with a new
> name [nature] written on the stone which no one knows
> except him who receives it.

Before erecting a building, the cornerstone must be accurately laid. It determines all the angles of the walls. Jesus had
been a carpenter in his younger days, if not a building contrac-
tor, and he understood this clearly. For the ancients had a com-

pletely trustworthy method of determining a right angle, which builders still use today. Ervin Seale gives a vital clue by relating our text to the following geometric axiom: The square of the hypotenuse of a right-angle triangle is equal to the sum of the squares of the other two sides.[13] This is called Euclid's 47th Proposition, and its discovery is also attributed to Pythagoras. Even the Sumerians, however, who flourished in 2000 B.C. and still earlier, applied this knowledge to their extensive building activities.

Forming a belief structure without the cornerstone is like putting up a building with crooked walls. The disordered stresses in such a house will certainly lead to its collapse. Similarly, to symbolically "kill" the son is to turn from the Christ within, and thus destroy one's own character.

As with anything discordant, however, this destructive process is self-limiting and must ultimately fail—for the Son is eternal and cannot really be destroyed. The Christ stands as a true cornerstone, despite all the error, confusion, and fear that the individual soul has accepted. Jesus tells us that we can begin again upon a true, faithful, and enduring basis. Every false concept is dissolved before it. The vineyard is restored and made productive. Its fruits are no longer wild and bitter, but cultivated and wholesome. The new wine of spiritual consciousness is again produced and made our own.

Affirmations

The indwelling Christ is the true cornerstone of my soul.

I invite God's perfect ideas to function through me in mind and body.

False beliefs, habits, and attitudes are dissolved into their native nothingness.

Praise God! His perfect ideas have reclaimed the vineyard of my soul.

Section V—
PARABLES OF
FORGIVENESS

Paul said...in Second Corinthians, "God is in Christ, no longer holding our misdeeds against us." The most radical of *all* notions. *No* exceptions. *No* condition. Now, I wouldn't have done it that way. I would have had a lot of exceptions. But it's not there.... Jesus doesn't say I come to proclaim release of captives unless they're Kluxers or unless they're blacks.... And when you couple that information with an earlier passage from the same chapter of Second Corinthians, a passage that says we no longer judge or see anyone by human standards, even though once we did—well, you're dealing in something radical. If you can stop judging folks by human standards, then you've gotten rid of a considerable load.[1]

—*Will Campbell*

The word "forgive" in the teachings of Jesus covers far more ground than its common usage indicates. It means vastly more than forgiving someone for a past injury, or some fault. Forgiveness includes a new way of viewing God, people, the earth, and ourselves. It is an awakening to the truth that God is All and in all, and to the power of this realization in thought and action.

Jesus' parables cannot be placed in strict categories, and the sections in this book are merely for convenience sake. All of his parables point to an advance beyond settled boundaries of thought. They lead to an expanded vision of reality, of individual potential, and of personal relations. Yet some reveal with special clarity how the attitude of forgiveness brings grace and

119

freedom, and how its absence maintains bondage to karma and limitation.

The healing, harmonizing, restoring power of divine love is here and now. The forgiving power of divine love is ready to heal our own sense of fear and guilt. The master Teacher showed how this power can be accepted, released, and called forth through the individual. This is the inner dynamic of the teaching to love one another, to pray for one's enemies, and to forgive all. Herein lies the remedy for violence of all kinds, and the prospect for peace on earth.

Chapter 23

The Lost Sheep

³So he told them this parable: ⁴"'What man of you, having a hundred sheep, if he has lost one of them, does not leave the ninety-nine in the wilderness, and go after the one which is lost, until he finds it? ⁵And when he has found it, he lays it on his shoulders, rejoicing. ⁶And when he comes home, he calls together his friends and his neighbors, saying to them, 'Rejoice with me, for I have found my sheep which was lost.' [⁷Just so, I tell you, there will be more joy in heaven over one sinner who repents than over ninety-nine righteous persons who need no repentance.]"
—Luke 15:3–7

Jesus said, "The kingdom is like a shepherd who had a hundred sheep. One of them, the largest, went astray. He left the ninety-nine and looked for that one until he found it. When he had gone to such trouble, he said to the sheep, 'I care for you more than the ninety-nine.' "
—Thomas 107 (parallel passage: Matthew 18:12–14)

The imagery of the shepherd and sheep was widespread in the ancient world. It is prominent in the Judeo-Christian tradition. To this day, more people know the 23rd Psalm than any other part of the Bible with the possible exception of the Lord's Prayer. This accounts for the potency of these images, deeply buried in the consciousness of many generations, to influence humanity down through the ages. The shepherd-sheep symbology extended to Egypt, Greece, and beyond. Aries the Ram is one of the twelve signs of the zodiac. The title of the *Poimandres*, an old Hermetic work, means "Shepherd of Men."

The good shepherd evolved as an archetype of the Christ-self. In John 10:11,14, Jesus declares: "I am the good shepherd."

In Greece, at a still earlier time, some artists depicted the legendary Orpheus as a good shepherd. They pictured animals of various kinds—not sheep alone—standing around him peacefully in a circle. This means that as we become identified with the indwelling Christ, the inner forces of mind and body are harmonized and uplifted around this central focus.

To document all the ancient uses of the shepherd and the sheep is beyond the scope of this chapter. It would require a book in itself. Also, the widespread use of this imagery makes it difficult to draw the boundaries of what Jesus intended by the parable of the lost sheep. It is easy to claim too little, or too much. It is best to treat it as open-ended, and to welcome its many facets of meaning.

Part of our challenge is that Matthew and Luke give different settings for the parable of the lost sheep. The gospel of Matthew presents it as a call to seek out Christians who have fallen away from the church. According to the gospel of Luke, however, Jesus gave the parable in response to complaints by the scribes and Pharisees that he receives sinners and eats with them. The gospel of Thomas provides no context at all, but merely begins it with the statement, "Jesus said."

Matthew 18:14 concludes its version:

So it is not the will of my Father who is in heaven that one of these little ones should perish.

On the other hand, Luke 15:7 reads:

Just so, I tell you, there will be more joy in heaven over one sinner who repents than over ninety-nine righteous persons who need no repentance.

These statements are too different to go back to a common source, and thus are probably later additions to the parable. Also, Thomas has no trace of a generalized ending. In addition, the parable's context in Matthew obviously reflects a later situation. Jesus would not have meant, as its proximity to Matthew 18:15–17 implies, that Christian leaders should make an effort to bring persons who had left the church back into "the fold."

This was, of course, a valid concern of the later church and appropriate to include in a manual such as the gospel of Matthew. There was, however, no organized Christian movement during Jesus' ministry on earth. The church had its earliest beginnings after the ascension, at Pentecost. Moreover, the gospels make no mention of any effort by Jesus to seek out ex-disciples. He kept busy day and night ministering to those who *wanted* healing and instruction.

The gospel of Luke, on the other hand, *may* reflect at least one of the original settings for this parable. The Pharisees were noted for the classes of people whom they held in contempt. They directed their strongest feelings against those whom Jesus made a point of welcoming, including harlots, tax-gatherers, and peasants. Thus, the Pharisees might have motivated Jesus to present a story in which he, as a symbolic shepherd, sought out a lost sheep.

All three accounts mention one hundred sheep, and all make the point that the man left ninety-nine sheep behind to search for the lost animal. A commentary on the parable, in the Valentinian *Gospel of Truth* (approx. 150 A.D.), agrees: "He is the shepherd who left behind him the ninety-nine sheep which had not strayed. He went, he sought after that one which had strayed. He rejoiced when he found it."[2] Taken in combination, this is conclusive evidence that the original parable included one hundred and ninety-nine.

There are two reasons for attributing importance to these totals, and they reinforce one another. One reason is sociological. George Lamsa explained that owning at least one hundred sheep has a prestige value:

> Most Easterners either have one hundred sheep or strive to get that number. A man with a hundred sheep is considered well to do and content.... The desire to have a hundred sheep is so strong that no one would like to see the number of his sheep fall below that figure. Therefore, when a man who has one hundred sheep loses one of them, he is more concerned over it than the man who had only seventy-five and lost even five. This is because no fami-

ly wants to see the number of their sheep fall below the coveted figure.[3]

The other reason is numerological. To the ancients, 10, 100, and 1000 were symbolic expansions of the number 1. (From the standpoint of numerology, $99/9+9=18/1+8=9$, but $100/1+0+0=1$.) The number 1 meant God as the totality of being. Thus, the loss of one sheep from the herd of one hundred signifies a loss of totality or wholeness. The stray sheep must be reunited with the other ninety-nine in order to restore harmony and completeness.

The basic theme of the parable of the lost sheep (and also the lost coin in Luke 15:8-9) is thus making whole what is, or has become, incomplete. This follows from the transition between ninety-nine and one hundred. Elizabeth Boyden Howes, commenting on the psychological aspects, declares:

> In these parables the owner has ten coins or one hundred sheep and places great value on this fact, so much so that each owner goes out in search of what is lost. We likewise must cherish and protect the totality of what is given within us. Loss of any part of our wholeness will damage the whole and therefore the lost must be redeemed. Psychologically this involves pursuing unconscious parts of ourselves that have been split off from consciousness and could remain quite autonomous and not contribute to the whole.[4]

As already stated, however, the parable of the lost sheep is broad and open-ended. It can be taken on at least four levels within the larger theme of wholeness:

First, the creative work of divine Mind is instantaneous and complete. Yet, until all people are fully awakened to their divine nature, God's work is paradoxically incomplete. Until then, the purpose of creation remains only partially fulfilled. Thus we read of a cosmic plan:

> For the creation waits with eager longing for the revealing of the sons of God...the creation itself will be set free from

its bondage to decay and obtain the glorious liberty of the children of God (Romans 8:19,21).

"For he has made known to us in all wisdom and insight the mystery of his will, according to his purpose which he set forth in Christ as a plan for the fullness of time, to unite all things in him, things in heaven and things on earth" (Ephesians 1:9–10).

For from him and through him and to him are all things.
To him be glory for ever (Romans 11:36).

At the very heart of being is that divine love which takes the initiative in reconciling humanity with itself. God does not wait for us to come to him. As the shepherd in the parable, *he seeks us out by inspiring us to respond positively to his ideas, to the movement of the divine life, love, and wisdom within us.* At its core, it is a case of God seeking humanity, rather than humanity seeking God. In this sense, universal Mind is the good shepherd.

Second, in a derived sense Jesus is the good shepherd. As an historical person, he realized with unique clarity—unmatched in the history of religious thought—that God's action within us precedes any human response or cooperation with the divine purpose, which is unlimited good. God seeks us out first, offering inward renewal and, with it, the key to the solution of every human problem.

This does not imply that humanity is evil by nature, or incapable of good. Rather, it affirms that God is all-in-all, and that humanity is God in expression, inseparably one with this allness. Thus, in seeking out the lost, Jesus demonstrated God's infinite love toward every person. He made a point of going to those who were most critically in need of help, giving less attention to those relatively well-off, morally and spiritually.

Third, the indwelling Christ is the good shepherd. The Christ, God's idea of himself within us, shepherds our individual thoughts, emotions, attitudes, and beliefs. The sheep that needs rescue is any thought or image that is cut off from the action of the mind of Christ. Whatever is false or errant needs to be rescued, cared for, and restored to the integrity of the whole flock.

Fourth, and in keeping with Dr. Howes' commentary, this process cannot work freely without our conscious consent. Thus, we too are shepherds on an individual level. When, acting from our conscious mind and will, we become aware of a "lost" area in our psyche, we bring the indwelling Christ to bear upon it. Then the negative factor is transformed into a positive one, like the legendary frog who becomes a prince. This is self-forgiveness in action, by which we realize our wholeness or completeness.

A final point is that of *joy.* Matthew, Luke, and the Gospel of Truth affirm joy, and Thomas' version implies it. This reminds us that Jesus' teachings are essentially joyful. They not only release a joyful state within the soul; they provide reasons for rejoicing. On whatever level we view this parable, we find that disease gives way to health, disharmony yields to harmony, and error is replaced by truth. This is forgiveness in the larger sense of the word.

Affirmations

I rejoice in the vision of God completing his work in and through me.

I rejoice in the vision of God completing his work in and through all people everywhere.

I rejoice in the indwelling Christ, working within my soul as wholeness, harmony, and well-being.

I fully agree with the indwelling action of God, bringing order, harmony, and fulfillment into all my experiences.

===

Chapter 24

The Lost Coin

[8]"Or what woman, having ten silver coins, if she loses one coin, does not light a lamp and sweep the house and seek diligently until she finds it? [9]And when she has found it, she calls together her friends and neighbors, saying, 'Rejoice with me, for I have found the coin which I had lost.' [[10]Just so, I tell you, there is joy before the angels of God over one sinner who repents.]"

–Luke 15:8–10

The parables of the lost sheep and the lost coin occur together in the gospel of Luke, but not in Matthew and Thomas. If Jesus gave them in sequence, as shown in Luke, he did so to convey a more restrictive meaning than was possible with the figures of a shepherd and a lost sheep. As Jesus was male, he could reasonably hope that his hearers would not identify the woman in the parable with him. On occasion, he called himself the good shepherd, but never the good housewife. Such a metaphor simply would not fit. A woman, however, was an accepted symbol for the individual soul. It is in this direction that the correct interpretation can be found.

Nevertheless, some early Christians later identified the woman in the parable with Jesus. Note verse 10; its similarity to 15:7, following 15:1-2, shows that this was the case. As such a view is untenable, so is 15:10 as a context for our parable. (Incidentally, it is important to note here that the verse numbers were not part of the original text, and therefore have no bearing on the interpretation. They were added to the Bible during the middle ages.)

Given the significance of the number ten, numerology enters into the picture. Ten is a symbolic expansion of the num-

127

ber one, signifying wholeness or totality. Therefore, the loss of
one coin from a collection of ten suggests a loss of totality
which, however, is restored with the finding of the lost member.

Reviewing the ancient symbology of the number ten,
Edward F. Edinger states:

> The "holy of Holies" which contains the ark of the
> covenant is thus a cube 10 x 10 x 10 cubits.... This corre-
> sponds to a similar valuation by the Greeks. The
> Pythagorean Tetractys (1+2+3+4=10) was a most sacred
> amulet. Aristotle tells us that "as the number 10 is thought
> to be perfect [teleion] and to comprise the whole nature of
> numbers, they say that the bodies which move through the
> heavens are ten, but as the visible bodies are only nine, to
> meet this they invent a tenth—the 'counter-earth.' " The
> Pythagoreans set up a table of ten principles arranged as
> ten pairs of opposites. Jewish tradition perpetuated the
> sacredness of the number ten in many ways, notably in the
> ten Sephiroth of the Kabbala.[5]

The importance of the lost coin, also, exceeds its monetary value which is beside the point. Its main worth is as an
ornament with symbolic meaning. This goes beyond numerology alone. Referring to the language of body decoration, an article in the *National Geographic* documents that "in Africa...a single ornament may identify the wearer's social status, age group,
or exploits in love, battle, or daily life."[6] The same applies to
Palestine, Syria, and other parts of the traditional Near East. In
some areas, it is the custom for a married woman to wear ten
coins on her head-dress. This is part of her dowry, and she will
wear them at all times. In other locales, women string their
symbolic coins together in a necklace. To lose even one of them
is a serious matter, bringing dismay and even disgrace to one so
careless.

Specifically, the coins in question have to do with a
woman's marriage. To lose even one of the ten is a bad sign as
to the future of her relationship with her husband. In the symbology of the parable, then, the loss of a coin points to a psychological inharmony or imbalance that can restrict communi-

cation between the Christ self (husband) and the individual soul (wife).

The woman in the parable lights a lamp, sweeps the house, and looks for the coin until she finds it. This refers to the work that we are to do in our own "house" or consciousness. That is to say, the parable dramatizes the need to bring the light of truth into the dark areas of the psyche. Also, we have to sweep away the mental dirt to recover what has been lost or dissociated. Then it can be restored to the integrity of the Christ mind in us.

The result of her success is joy and celebration. This reflects a psychological fact: When a dissociated area in the psyche is reintegrated and made whole, energy that had been siphoned off is restored. Soul and body are healed; what was incomplete is again made complete. At the same time, we feel joy, peace, and vitality welling up from within.

Toward these ends, various methods can be used, including meditation, affirmation, and visualization. God's grace is the prime mover to establish healing within and without. Nevertheless, we have our own work to do in clearing the path for the indwelling Spirit to function more fully in and through us. This is the spirit of Jesus' words in John 5:17: "My Father is working still, and I am working."

Affirmations

I forgive all false beliefs and images. I am poised, centered, and unified in the mind of Christ.

I am restored to wholeness within and without, through the presence and power of the indwelling Christ.

Chapter 25

The Two Debtors

³⁶One of the Pharisees asked him to eat with him, and he went into the Pharisee's house, and sat at table. ³⁷And behold, a woman of the city, who was a sinner, when she learned that he was sitting at table in the Pharisee's house, brought an alabaster flask of ointment, ³⁸and standing behind him at his feet, weeping, she began to wet his feet with her tears, and wiped them with the hair of her head, and kissed his feet, and anointed them with the ointment. ³⁹Now when the Pharisee who had invited him saw it, he said to himself, "If this man were a prophet, he would have known who and what sort of woman this is who is touching him, for she is a sinner." ⁴⁰And Jesus answering said to him, "Simon, I have something to say to you." And he answered, "What is it, Teacher?" ⁴¹"A certain creditor had two debtors; one owed five hundred denarii, and the other fifty. ⁴²When they could not pay, he forgave them both. Now which of them will love him more?" ⁴³Simon answered, "The one, I suppose, to whom he forgave more." And he said to him, "You have judged rightly." ⁴⁴Then turning toward the woman he said to Simon, "Do you see this woman? I entered your house; you gave me no water for my feet, but she has wet my feet with her tears and wiped them with her hair. ⁴⁵You gave me no kiss, but from the time I [the original Aramaic can be translated "she"] came in she has not ceased to kiss my feet. ⁴⁶You did not anoint my head with oil, but she has anointed my feet with ointment. ⁴⁷Therefore I tell you, her sins, which are many, are forgiven, for she loved much; but he who is forgiven little, loves little."

—Luke 7:36–47

The short parable in Luke 7:41–42 is closely integrated with its setting, and can be best understood in relation to it.[7] The text's cast of characters is as follows:

Simon the Pharisee—He invites Jesus to attend a banquet at his house. This he does out of shallow curiosity rather than sincere interest. He is civil to his guest, but gives him a minimum of attention.

Jesus—He receives the woman who washes, anoints, and kisses his feet. Simon objects to this, partly because Jesus is untroubled about being "defiled" by this woman's touch (7:39). Jesus responds with the parable in 7:41–42.

The Woman—Evidently a harlot, tradition identifies her with Mary Magdalene. There is no proof of this, but Mary is mentioned again in Luke 8:2 as one "from whom seven demons had gone out." She lavishes attention on Jesus, not for display but from the fullness of her gratitude to him as a spiritual healer and guide. She is unconcerned about the spectacle she is making of herself.

Jesus' words to Simon (7:44–46) will appear strange to an American or some Europeans. We don't expect a man to greet his male guest with a kiss, nor will he anoint him with oil or offer water for foot-washing. This, however, was accepted practice in the Near East and showed respect and affection for a guest. Also, people wore sandals and needed water to wash the dust off their feet.

Forgiveness is the basic theme of this parable. Jesus understood that the power to dissolve sin, fear, and everything negative is within the individual. In Simon's case, however, it was locked away from awareness or, we can say, dissociated. *Forgiveness is something we do primarily for ourselves, to maintain our conscious attunment with the infinite.* Conversely, to limit forgiveness is to limit one's own spiritual progress, and this was Simon's basic problem. He saw the woman in terms of her past mistakes, rather than as a soul struggling toward the light.

Simon, then, is a symbol of the intellect when ruled by dogmatism and self-righteousness. The woman, in her veneration of Jesus, represents creative imagination focused on one's own higher potential. *Jesus* represents the I AM or indwelling Christ, which is that higher potential.

The woman became released and healed from her dishonorable past as she focused on Jesus' positive qualities. Sometimes one person can serve another's needs in this way in the short term. This must not, however, become a long-lasting substitute for one's own spiritual and personal development. All that the woman perceived within the depths of Jesus' spirituality was really within herself, waiting to be called forth into awareness.

Both Simon and the woman needed forgiveness. The woman needed to be cleansed of her sins, and Simon of what he considered to be his virtues. For in refusing to forgive, Simon became a victim of his own anger and resentment. Also, the fact that he did nothing to serve Jesus means that one with this attitude does nothing to serve the Christ in himself or in others. He was too engrossed in error to allow that dynamic reality to heal and inspire him. Simon did no harm to the woman, but he banished himself from the kingdom of God, which is Oneness. John Sanford, commenting on this parable, writes:

> Evil is separation. Theologically, it is separation from God. Psychologically, it is separation within oneself. The kingdom of God comes to restore unity to man, to unify him with God and with himself.[8]

There is something to be said for the traditional distinction made between self-righteousness and divine righteousness:

> Indeed I count everything as loss because of the surpassing worth of knowing Christ Jesus my Lord. For his sake I have suffered the loss of all things, and count them as refuse, in order that I may gain Christ and be found in him, not having a righteousness of my own, based on law, but that which is through faith in Christ, the righteousness from God that depends on faith; that I may know him and the power of his resurrection.
>
> —Philippians 3:8–10

The woman served Jesus with ardor, even with abandon. She wet his feet with her tears, dried them with her hair, anointed them with ointment, and kissed them repeatedly. Whoever loves and gives steady attention to his or her own higher potential, the Christ, will also be lifted out of what is false, negative, and limiting. Jesus expressed the issue succinctly: Simon loved little and was forgiven little. The woman loved much, and was forgiven much.

Affirmations

I am willing to, and now forgive everyone, totally and without conditions.

I am willing to, and now forgive myself, totally and without conditions.

I focus on the mind of Christ and its perfect ideas. I am the Christ in conscious expression.

The love of Christ is now released in and through me, cleansing, healing, and adjusting my feelings and attitudes.

Chapter 26

The Unmerciful Servant

²³"Therefore the kingdom of heaven may be compared to a king who wished to settle accounts with his servants. ²⁴When he began the reckoning, one was brought to him who owed him ten thousand talents; ²⁵and as he could not pay, his lord ordered him to be sold, with his wife and children and all that he had, and payment to be made. ²⁶So the servant fell on his knees, imploring him, 'Lord, have patience with me, and I will pay you everything.' ²⁷And out of pity for him the lord of that servant released him and forgave him the debt. ²⁸But that same servant, as he went out, came upon one of his fellow servants who owed him a hundred denarii; and seizing him by the throat he said, 'Pay what you owe.' ²⁹So his fellow servant fell down and besought him, 'Have patience with me, and I will pay you.' ³⁰He refused and went and put him in prison till he should pay the debt. ³¹When his fellow servants saw what had taken place, they were greatly distressed, and they went and reported to their lord all that had taken place. ³²Then his lord summoned him and said to him, 'You wicked servant! I forgave you all that debt because you besought me; ³³and should not you have had mercy on your fellow servant, as I had mercy on you?' ³⁴And in anger his lord delivered him to the jailers, till he should pay all his debt. [³⁵So also my heavenly Father will do to every one of you, if you do not forgive your brother from your heart.]" —*Matthew 18:23–35*

Must there not be certain boundaries on our forgiveness? If someone hurts me physically or psychologically, I should forgive that person. However, if that blow or insult is repeated again and again, what are the limits of my forgiveness? This is a question that often troubles people seeking to do right in their personal relationships.

Peter's question precedes this parable: "Lord, how often shall my brother sin against me, and I forgive him? As many as seven times?" (Matthew 18:21). In the Jewish tradition, it is an established policy to forgive a person three times, but not a fourth time. Peter probably thought himself generous when he proposed forgiving someone up to seven times. Jesus, however, replied: "I do not say to you seven times, but seventy times seven" (18:22).

The point of Jesus' reply in 18:22 is unlimited forgiveness, which "seventy times seven" implies. This is followed, in 18:23-27, by the virtually unlimited forgiveness of the king for his servant. Therefore, the link between Peter's question and this parable is probably original. Verse 35, however, was added later. Jesus would not have proposed that human beings extend unlimited forgiveness if he believed that God the Father was angry and vindictive, and limited in forgiveness. It would be unbridled arrogance to claim to follow a higher standard than our divine Creator.

Considering the structure of Matthew 18 as a whole, the church in Antioch—where the gospel of Matthew was compiled between 70 and 100 A.D.—apparently faced a divisive situation at the time. This is not at all surprising, given the diverse beliefs of the early Christians in Syria. In all likelihood, the author sought to deal with a level of anger and hostility which had become a serious threat to the health of the church. This gave him a motive for adding a warning such as 18:35.

It is true that in Matthew 6:14-15, Jesus declares:

> For if you forgive men their trespasses, your heavenly Father also will forgive you; but if you do not forgive men their trespasses, neither will your Father forgive your trespasses.

Nevertheless, the point of this statement is different. In 6:14-15, forgiveness is not withheld because the Father is angry, or desires to withhold it. Forgiveness is withheld because an individual who refuses to forgive others is, by that very act of refusal, blocking the flow of forgiveness into his or her own soul. It is not a question of punishment, but of cause and effect, of action and reaction. Divine Mind has set this law into motion in such a way that it enforces itself.

Turning to the parable itself, we find that the servant owed his king ten thousand talents. This is extravagant imagery. In fact, at a conservative estimate, it amounted to at least $25,000,000! No servant, with limited credit, would have had a chance to incur such a ridiculous debt. It would have been difficult for the king, with access to the royal treasury, to have gone so deeply into the hole. In the parable, of course, the servant owed the king ten thousand talents, not the other way around. It is equally obvious that the servant had no real hope of paying the debt.

Note how Jesus used the datival introduction: "It is the case with the kingdom of heaven as with a king who wished to settle accounts with his servants." The parable, therefore, compares the coming of the kingdom with its end result, i.e. the cancellation of this enormous debt. His lord was about to sell him, his wife, and his children into slavery, but he ended up forgiving the entire sum.

A fellow servant owed this man one hundred denarii—no more than one hundred dollars in modern money. This is a trifling amount compared with the ten thousand talents. Nevertheless, the one hundred denarii was a substantial sum for a poor servant, but an amount that, with sustained effort, he could reasonably save and pay back. Despite this, the villain of the story grabbed him by the throat and demanded payment. When he didn't get it, he put the man in prison.

When his lord found out about this, he gave the offending servant the same treatment. Behind the bars of the jail, he lost any hope of being able to pay his debt. While in prison, he couldn't earn money; and without earning money, he couldn't get out of prison.

The unmerciful servant had a choice. At first, he appealed to his lord's mercy and was forgiven. Later, by refusing to forgive his own debtor, he subjected himself to the demands of strict justice. Had he forgiven his debtor, his own debts would have remained canceled. But in the parable, he did not do so and thus received the same punishment.

Exodus 21:2–25 is usually interpreted as an Old Testament ethical standard, based on equal and limited revenge. While this is part of the text's meaning, it also expresses the law of cause and effect:

> If any harm follows, then you shall give life for life, eye for eye, tooth for tooth, hand for hand, foot for foot, burn for burn, wound for wound, stripe for stripe.

There are, then, two realms of law under which an individual may choose to live. One is the realm of karma, of cause and effect, action and reaction. Unforgiveness and material attachments bind the soul to past mistakes and their results. It is like being against a stone wall with no way over or around; so it was with the man who was thrown into prison until he paid his debt.

The law of karma, however, is a mere counterfeit in relation to the kingdom of God. The way of escape is an awakening to the universal laws of Spirit. Herein God is perfect cause, and man as the Christ is perfect effect, inseparably one with the divine Father-Mother. God is the one presence and the one power, who forgives all errors, heals all diseases, and adjusts all things into harmony and order.

No one can be forgiven unless he or she is willing to forgive. This means forgiving others, forgiving and accepting oneself, and forgiving false and limiting beliefs of every kind. We cannot invite divine love into our consciousness, and block it at the same time by resentment and unforgiveness. We can have it one way or the other, but not both ways. Emmet Fox, discussing the Lord's Prayer, sums up the issue in a few words:

> He [Jesus] obliges us to declare that we have actually forgiven, and forgiven all, *and he makes our claim to our own forgiveness to depend upon that*...we cannot demand our own release before we have released our brother.[9]

Affirmations

I fully and freely forgive everyone.

I fully and freely forgive myself, and accept myself totally.

I fully and freely let go of all error.

I am willing to receive new ideas and new insights.

I am willing to awaken into the perfect realm of grace, where God is All-in-all.

Divine love is now active within me, establishing its own health, harmony, and wholeness in my experience.

Chapter 27

The Throne Claimant

¹²He said therefore, "A nobleman went into a far country to receive kingly power and then return. [¹³Calling ten of his servants, he gave them ten pounds, and said to them, 'Trade with these till I come.'] ¹⁴But his citizens hated him and sent an embassy after him, saying, 'We do not want this man to reign over us.' ¹⁵When he returned, having received the kingly power, [he commanded these servants, to whom he had given the money, to be called to him, that he might know what they had gained by trading. ¹⁶The first came before him, saying, 'Lord, your pound has made ten pounds more.' ¹⁷And he said to him, 'Well done, good servant! Because you have been faithful in a very little, you shall have authority over ten cities.' ¹⁸And the second came, saying, 'Lord, your pound has made five pounds.' ¹⁹And he said to him, 'And you are to be over five cities.' ²⁰Then another came, saying, 'Lord, here is your pound, which I have kept laid away in a napkin; ²¹for I was afraid of you, because you are a severe man; you take up what you did not lay down, and reap what you did not sow.' ²²He said to him, 'I will condemn you out of your own mouth, you wicked servant! You knew that I was a severe man, taking up what I did not lay down and reaping what I did not sow? ²³Why then did you not put my money into the bank, and at my coming I should have collected it with interest?' ²⁴And he said to those who stood by, 'Take the pound from him, and give it to him who has the ten pounds.' ²⁵(And they said to him, 'Lord, he has ten pounds!') ²⁶I tell you, that to every one who has will more be given; but from him who has not, even what he has will be taken away.] ²⁷But as for these enemies of mine, who did not want me to reign over them, bring them here and slay them before me.'"

–Luke 19:12–27

The major note of this parable is in accord with the teachings of Jesus; the more we give in love to others, the greater the results, and our abilities to help will be multiplied. The minor note, the ruthlessness of judgment upon those who withhold their talents, their abilities, leads us to make a careful examination of this passage.

This passage is sometimes called the parable of the pounds. In the original text, the actual monetary unit is the *mina*. It was worth many times more than today's British pound sterling.

As already noted in Chapter 18, Luke 19:12-27 combines two parables. The author of Luke would have had a purpose of his own in doing so. Luke 19:11, which introduces this text, states that Jesus "proceeded to tell a parable, because he was near to Jerusalem." Evidently the author altered his text to relate the parable to Jesus' prediction that the Jewish authorities in Jerusalem would be overthrown. And, at the time of writing (after 70 A.D.), the Romans had already pillaged Jerusalem and destroyed the temple.

By comparing Luke 19:12-27 with the parable of the talents in Matthew 25:14-29, we find that three passages are clearly intrusive. Specifically, these are Luke 19:12, 14-15a, and 27. Taken in combination, they yield the following text:

> "A nobleman went into a far country to receive kingly power and then return.... But his citizens hated him and sent an embassy after him, saying, 'We do not want this man to reign over us.' When he returned, having received the kingly power[...] 'But as for these enemies of mine, who did not want me to reign over them, bring them here and slay them before me.' "

This is the core of another parable, which we will call *the throne claimant*. We do not have its full text, for something is omitted between 19:15a and 19:27.

Based upon what remains, it is likely that Jesus referred to actual history—though not to the fall of Jerusalem—and based a lesson upon it. It accords well with another sequence of events: When Herod the Great died in 4 B.C. (some scholars date this event in 1 B.C.), a son, Archelaus, inherited his throne. He went to Rome to have his kingship confirmed by Octavian, who had become Emperor Caesar Augustus. The emperor, however, was pulled two ways. Since Herod the Great had been consistently loyal to Rome, and rewarding loyal service was part of Augustus' code of honor, in a sense it seemed right to grant Archelaus' request. On the other hand, he had information which cast serious doubt upon Archelaus' fitness to rule. So Augustus decided on a compromise. Archelaus received about half of Herod's realm, including Judea, Samaria, and Idumea, but had to be content with the title of *ethnarch*, which had a lower rank than *king*.

The text also alludes to a delegation of Judeans who traveled to Rome to oppose his confirmation. Evidently they came not with a reasoned petition, but in a hateful and vindictive spirit. They deeply resented the excesses of Herod's prior reign, and therefore reacted against his son. Though their position had merit, when they appealed to Augustus in a negative way, they probably hurt their own case. Also, after Archelaus came to power, he responded in kind, severely punishing his enemies.

Jesus meant that hate and revenge produce more of the same, and redound to the offender. The person verbally or physically attacked will not retaliate in every case; but if not, a third party will do so. This is a self-enforcing law of cause and effect, of action and reaction. Incidentally, in 6 A.D. Archelaus was removed from office, and his territories placed under direct Roman rule.

Of course, the law also works positively. Love and good will produce more of the same, and return to bless the individual. Again, the object of loving attention will not respond in every case, but others will. What we give out comes back to us, which is good news if what we are giving out is good, and bad news if it is not. The way to have more love, joy, peace, and wisdom is thus to radiate these qualities to others.

Affirmations

I am the living expression of divine LOVE. I radiate love to others.

I am the living expression of the JOY of the Lord. I radiate joy to others.

I am the living expression of God's PEACE. I radiate peace to others.

I am the living expression of Christ WISDOM. I radiate wisdom to others.

The blessings that God expresses through me return to me multiplied.

Chapter 28

The Pharisee and the Publican

⁹He also told this parable to some who trusted in themselves that they were righteous and despised others: ¹⁰"Two men went up into the temple to pray, one a Pharisee and the other a tax collector. ¹¹The Pharisee stood and prayed thus with himself, 'God, I thank thee that I am not like other men, extortioners, unjust, adulterers, or even like this tax collector. ¹²I fast twice a week, I give tithes of all that I get.' ¹³But the tax collector, standing far off, would not even lift up his eyes to heaven, but beat his breast, saying, 'God, be merciful to me a sinner!' ¹⁴I tell you, this man went down to his house justified rather than the other; for every one who exalts himself will be humbled, but he who humbles himself will be exalted."

—Luke 18:9–14

In this brief, striking parable Jesus cuts through our self-satisfaction and pride. In drawing a simple word picture of two contrasting personalities, he causes us to question the authenticity of our faith. Is our self-image an indication of true holiness, or is it vanity?

Scholars have questioned whether the concluding proverb belongs in this context: "for every one who exalts himself will be humbled, but he who humbles himself will be exalted." Its presence is not supported by independent evidence, as is the case with the chief seats (Luke 14:7–11). On balance, however, it seems correct to retain it here. The Pharisee in the parable displays an egoistic sense of separation and superiority. (The word "Pharisee," in fact, means "separated.") Also, the parable expands on the tradition of the book of Proverbs, where we find passages such as:

When pride comes, then comes disgrace;
    but with the humble is wisdom.

                        —Proverbs 11:2

Pride goes before destruction,
    and a haughty spirit before a fall.

                      —Proverbs 16:18

A man's pride will bring him low,
    but he who is lowly in spirit will obtain honor.

                      —Proverbs 29:23

The publican's saving grace was his lack of pretense as he faced what was false in himself, coupled with an honest sense of need. This enabled him to get back in tune with the infinite. By humbling himself, he was exalted.

Before we comment further on what this parable means, it is needful to say what it is not. Its intent is *not* to show that the Pharisee was wrong because he thought well of himself, and that the tax collector was right because he declared himself to be a sinner. Our text is not a commentary on "human nature" in a theological sense. It *is* a way of portraying two states of consciousness. One opens the door to forgiveness, and the other closes it. Obviously, the goal is to advance beyond *both* attitudes portrayed in the parable, so as to realize wholeness.

He also told this parable to some who trusted in themselves that they were righteous and despised others(18:9).

This translation fails to convey the impact of Luke's Greek. They trusted in themselves *because* (*hoti* in Greek) they were righteous. The text also clearly implies that those who "trusted in themselves" did so in direct contrast to those who trust in God. They trusted in themselves to the exclusion of, and even in opposition to, such a trust. This is the reverse of the positive self-trust that *grows out of trust in God*. Their "confidence"—for whatever it was worth—rested in personal conformity to their own code of conduct, rather than in any sense of the divine presence at work in their lives.

The Greek text also conveys the meaning that they had *a settled conviction* that they were superior. They had convinced themselves—or, in modern usage, *programmed* themselves—into a confirmed attitude. This outlook included not only spiritual pride, but severe contempt for those who did not share their opinions.

Two men went up into the temple to pray, one a Pharisee and the other a tax collector (18:10).

The Pharisees and the publicans were at opposite poles in the opinion of society. This does not mean that every Pharisee was like the one in the parable, for we must always allow for individual differences. They did, however, in general, and increasingly over a span of time, manifest certain tendencies to which the gospels validly point.

The Pharisees were a sect who were regarded as ideal examples of the Jewish religion. They scrupulously practiced the letter of the law. In addition, they practiced ceremonial hand washing and other customs not required by the Torah. They were so focused on externals, however, that they lost sight of the inner life of the Spirit. This is reflected in Matthew 23:25–26, where Jesus became unusually severe:

> Woe to you, scribes and Pharisees, hypocrites! for you cleanse the outside of the cup and of the plate, but inside they are full of extortion and rapacity. You blind Pharisee! first cleanse the inside of the cup and of the plate, that the outside also may be clean.

If the Pharisee denoted public esteem, the publican (shown here as "tax collector") denoted treason. In a republic, the tax collector has a legitimate function. In Judea, however, he made his living by collecting taxes—in cash or in kind—for the Romans. They, in turn, used the proceeds both to finance their occupation and to enrich the treasury in Rome. What is more, though he collected taxes from his fellow Jews, he received no salary; he made a profit by charging more than the Romans required. For example, if a given village had to supply fifty sheep, he would try to get seventy-five or one hundred and keep the difference. The Romans didn't care, as long as they received their quota.

The Pharisee stood and prayed thus with himself, 'God, I thank thee that I am not like other men, extortioners, unjust, adulterers, or even like this tax collector' (18:11).

The statement that he prayed *with himself* is a basic clue to Jesus' intent. This Pharisee's so-called "goodness" was not grounded in spiritual communion, nor did he try to sense the image of God in himself or in others. He built his life on an arrogant attempt to lift himself up by putting others down. Note the negative nature of his comments: *extortioners, unjust, adulterers.*

He projected these sins on others, rather than face his own tendencies along the same lines. Yet with his rigid code of conduct, he would have avoided the overt acts. This is what Jesus meant by a whited sepulchre. It signifies an unwholesome mix of evil desires, bad thoughts about others, and suppression of negative actions. It amounts to a fatigued and fruitless spiritual condition.

'I fast twice a week, I give tithes of all that I get' (18:12).

One can rationalize such a state by saying, "After all, I have followed the rules." Our Pharisee fasted two days a week, though most people considered one day a week to be adequate. Also, he tithed faithfully—in itself a good and helpful practice. But, as Ervin Seale points out, he had frozen his spiritual development:

> The error of the Pharisee in this parable is that he justifies himself by his outward behavior, and this indicates complete ignorance of the law. The Pharisee, believing that he has arrived, is no longer teachable. He is bound at a certain level of development, for being unwilling to think a new thought, he cannot move into a new and higher level of himself.[10]

But the tax collector, standing far off, would not even lift up his eyes to heaven, but beat his breast, saying, 'God, be merciful to me a sinner!' (18:13).

This publican was hardly an exemplary character. We wonder what were his selfish acts, wasted years, which caused him to beat his breast with feelings that combined guilt and despair? Whatever his past, the good thing was that he now clearly knew he needed to change. He knew that this must be a change not only in outer behavior, but also in consciousness. Obviously he was free of the Pharisee's self-righteousness, pretense, and belief in his own adequacy apart from God. He now recognized his mistakes, knew he could do nothing apart from God, and was teachable. In such an agitated though receptive state, the Holy Spirit can enter a soul and make it whole.

I tell you, this man went down to his house justified rather than the other; for every one who exalts himself will be humbled, but he who humbles himself will be exalted (18:14).

Jesus intended that this parable would shock his hearers out of their complacency. He certainly didn't give them what they expected. The devout Pharisee's prayer resembles one found in the Talmud. At the time, it would have existed in oral tradition as a recommended prayer. The publican, in stark contrast, was a traitor to Israel. Yet the publican went to his house (a symbol for consciousness) restored to harmony with God— but not the Pharisee.

John D. Crossan correctly calls this a parable of *polar reversal*. He states: "The metaphorical challenge is...clear: the complete, radical, polar reversal of accepted human judgment, even or especially of religious judgment, whereby the Kingdom forces its way into human awareness."[11]

Affirmations

I renounce the illusion of separation from God.

I am open and receptive to the indwelling Spirit of God.

My trust is in the one presence, one mind, one power that is all.

Chapter 29

The Good Samaritan

[²⁵And behold, a lawyer stood up to put him to the test, saying, "Teacher, what shall I do to inherit eternal life?" ²⁶He said to him, "What is written in the law? How do you read?" ²⁷And he answered, "You shall love the Lord your God with all your heart, and with all your soul, and with all your strength, and with all your mind; and your neighbor as yourself." ²⁸And he said to him, "You have answered right; do this, and you will live."

²⁹But he, desiring to justify himself, said to Jesus, "And who is my neighbor?" ³⁰Jesus replied,] "A man was going down from Jerusalem to Jericho, and he fell among robbers, who stripped him and beat him, and departed, leaving him half dead. ³¹Now by chance a priest was going down that road; and when he saw him he passed by on the other side. ³²So likewise a Levite, when he came to the place and saw him, passed by on the other side. ³³But a Samaritan, as he journeyed, came to where he was; and when he saw him, he had compassion, ³⁴and went to him and bound up his wounds, pouring on oil and wine; then he set him on his own beast and brought him to an inn, and took care of him. ³⁵And the next day he took out two denarii and gave them to the innkeeper, saying, 'Take care of him; and whatever more you spend, I will repay you when I come back.' ³⁶Which of these three, do you think, proved neighbor to the man who fell among the robbers?" [³⁷He said, "The one who showed mercy on him." And Jesus said to him, "Go and do likewise."]

–Luke 10:25-37

Jesus' two great commandments, which the lawyer recites, appear in Luke 10:27:

148

You shall love the Lord your God with all your heart, and with all your soul, and with all your strength, and with all your mind; and your neighbor as yourself.

The two great commandments also appear in somewhat similar passages in Matthew 22:34-40 and Mark 12:28-31. There, however, Jesus himself declares them, not the lawyer mentioned in Luke 10:25. Yet neither Matthew nor Mark includes the parable of the good Samaritan. Also, both Matthew and Mark date this event between Palm Sunday and the last supper, whereas Luke claims an earlier point in time for it. Moreover, only Luke includes the lawyer's question: "And who is my neighbor?"

Therefore, it is likely that 10:25-28 and 10:30-35 derive from separate occasions in Jesus' ministry.[12] This linkage may be a product either of Luke himself, or of the tradition upon which he drew. The lawyer's question in Luke 10:29 is a literary device, a transition to join these two passages together.

This is one of the best known parables. In popular usage, a "good Samaritan" is one who helps another person in need. All would agree that love of God and love of neighbor are essential to Jesus' teaching. Not only is helping a neighbor in need the right thing to do, but the priest and Levite seem less than human when they leave the victim lying in the ditch. The Samaritan, in striking contrast, not only stops to aid the victim, but puts himself in some danger. The robbers might still have been nearby. In any case, the road from Jerusalem to Jericho was notorious for highway robbery—in the literal sense.

The parable looks simple on the surface, but there is much more to it than a cursory reading reveals. To sense its full impact, we must consider the historical enmity between Samaritans and Jews. The Samaritans, as a group, lived in the area bordered by Galilee and Phoenicia to the north and Judea to the south. They were a mixed race. When the northern kingdom of Israel fell to the Assyrian invaders in 722 B.C., the leaders among the ten tribes were deported. The common people remained, for the most part, but Assyrian settlers moved in and intermarried with them.

The Samaritans considered themselves to be true followers

of Moses and true keepers of the law. Yet the Judeans rejected them. There had been a long-standing, and at times violent, rivalry between the two factions which had persisted for many generations. The hatred increased with every hostile act, and finally culminated in the destruction of the Samaritan temple by John Hyrcanus, king of Judea (approximately 109 B.C.).

Many rabbis taught that if a Jew accepted help from a Samaritan, it would delay the redemption of Israel. Such a ridiculous prejudice shows the depth of ill will that existed. There was no forgiveness, then, between Samaritan and Jew. Jesus, however, reversed the entrenched attitude that Jewish priests and Levites were automatically good, and that Samaritans were as certainly bad. *In his parable, the priest and Levite become bad, and the Samaritan good.* By challenging his hearers' presumptions head-on, he made them question their mechanical sense of "good" and "bad." Also, he compelled them to consider the meaning of *forgiveness*, which includes beholding the divine presence in everyone and everything. The kingdom of God, which is conscious oneness, dissolves the false sense of dualism, separation, and hostility in whatever form it may exist. And, as Crossan declares, "The hearer struggling with the contradictory dualism of Good/Samaritan is actually experiencing in and through this the inbreaking of the Kingdom."[13]

The Samaritan, though in principle rejected by the Judean, brings him healing and rescue. The Samaritan binds up his wounds, using wine as a disinfectant and oil to promote healing. Then he sets him on a beast of burden, brings him to an inn, and takes care of him. When he leaves, he gives the innkeeper money, and promises to pay any additional expenses that the man might incur. This points to another level of meaning. The helper-victim relationship in the parable is like that between (1) the inner Messiah, the indwelling Christ, and (2) the individual mind and body. The good Samaritan, then, is the Christ, our own highest Self. On a personal level, we can reject our spiritual identity as the Jew spurned the Samaritan. Until we receive the healing Christ, however, we remain in a metaphoric ditch, half-dead because of our ignorance and false beliefs.

In the world of this parable, accepting the Samaritan's help brings a complete reversal of condition. His actions in Luke 10:34–35 are sufficient to show that he indeed represents the indwelling Christ. The robbers, being negative and destructive, are lawless thoughts and emotions. The priests and Levites do not help; they represent formal religion (of any persuasion) that fails to meet human needs. When the Christ is received into awareness, however, healing occurs. The eternal I AM and the personal I are reintegrated. This inner union "disinfects" us from every harmful influence, and brings the oil of healing to mind, body, and affairs. It is true forgiveness in action.

As readers, we can identify either with the helpful Samaritan, or with the victim who receives help. Either image involves the reader in the parable, and this is a positive step. Both figures point to aspects of our total being. Note, however, that the Samaritan solves the problem. This suggests the advantage of identifying not only with the rescued man, but also with the Christ self whom the Samaritan represents. The eventual result of this is total freedom, total healing, and total forgiveness.

Affirmations

I am an open channel for the free flow of God's life, light, and love.

I dedicate my whole being to God, and I am harmonized and healed.

Through divine love active in me, I love my neighbor as myself.

As I behold the divine presence in everyone and everything, I receive total forgiveness.

Light and joy and peace abide in me. My mind is poised in peace and beauty. I rest in calm trust, and rely on the indwelling Christ to bring good into my experience.

Section VI–
OBSTACLES ON
THE PATH

The parables in this section, with the possible exception of the rich fool, are not as well known as many of the others. Yet each has an important message. In one way or another, they outline the choice between drifting and inertia on the one hand, and a calm resolve to focus on the light of truth on the other hand. They affirm that what appear to be challenges and choices in the world of affairs are really occasions for our inner growth and progress.

The parables also go a long way toward giving us a true estimate of Jesus' consciousness and character. His biography has frequently been mishandled by religious leaders. Through his parables, however, correctly understood, the master Teacher can speak with a clear voice to today's world. The individual, and society in general, are much in need of his freeing insights into God's spiritual laws.

Chapter 30

The Rich Fool

[¹³One of the multitude said to him, "Teacher, bid my brother divide the inheritance with me." ¹⁴But he said to him, "Man, who made me a judge or divider over you?" ¹⁵And he said to them, "Take heed, and beware of all covetousness; for a man's life does not consist in the abundance of his possessions."] ¹⁶And he told them a parable, saying, "The land of a rich man brought forth plentifully; ¹⁷and he thought to himself, 'What shall I do, for I have nowhere to store my crops?' ¹⁸And he said, 'I will do this; I will pull down my barns, and build larger ones; and there I will store all my grain and my goods. ¹⁹And I will say to my soul, Soul, you have ample goods laid up for many years; take your ease, eat, drink, be merry.' ²⁰But God said to him, 'Fool! This night your soul is required of you; and the things you have prepared, whose will they be?' [²¹So is he who lays up treasure for himself, and is not rich toward God.]"

–Luke 12:13-21

Jesus said, "There was a rich man who had much money. He said, 'I shall put my money to use so that I may sow, reap, plant, and fill my storehouse with produce, with the result that I shall lack nothing.' Such were his intentions, but that same night he died. [Let him who has ears hear.]"

–Thomas 63

A comparison of Luke 12:13-21 with Saying 72 of the gospel of Thomas indicates that the passage in Luke is a literary composite. Verses 13–14, 15, and 16–20 all come from different situations. For verses 13–14 and 16–20 are linked by verse 15 in

Luke, but the gospel of Thomas lists the two passages separately. Whereas the parable appears in Thomas as Saying 63, Saying 72 reads:

> A man said to him, "Tell my brothers to divide my father's possessions with me."
> He said to him, "O man, who has made me a divider?"
> He turned to his disciples and said to them, "I am not a divider, am I?"

Verse 15 is authentic and well taken: "Take heed, and beware of all covetousness; for a man's life does not consist in the abundance of his possessions." At the same time, its linkage with the adjoining verses is not original. It is *not* self-evident that the brother demanding his inheritance was motivated by greed. It is at least as likely that he spoke from a sense of injustice. At any rate, the claimant's rights are the issue, not his emotional state. Also, regarding the rich man, greed would not have been the primary motive for his actions. If he had simply been greedy, he would not have decided to retire and indulge himself. He would have determined to work all the harder to gain more wealth, no matter how much he already had.

Verse 21 is also probably a later addition to the parable: "So is he who lays up treasure for himself, and is not rich toward God." Thomas omits this ending, though it would fit Thomas 63 more closely than it does Luke 12:16–20. Apparently the saying was not in the author of Thomas' source. Similarly, Luke's text makes no mention of the ending in Thomas: "Let him who has ears hear." Of course, this proverb is a "floater" which appears in a variety of contexts, both in Thomas and in the synoptic gospels. Luke 12:16–20 is thus the text to be interpreted, with Thomas 63 also to be considered except for the last sentence.

This parable, open-ended as it is, speaks to the reader on various levels. In one sense, and correctly so, it views *greed* for material goods as a deterrent to spiritual progress. Nevertheless, it makes no argument against wealth as such; and in fact, greed is an affirmation of lack rather than abundance.

The parable's primary intent is apparent in the key terms, *thought to himself* and *fool*. The man *thought to himself,* which means without reference to divine ideas and guidance. He made his own plans, without asking whether or not they were in accord with the divine purpose for his life. Also, a *fool* in the biblical sense is one who does not believe in God, or, if a formal believer, one who conducts his life *as if* there were no God. For example, Psalm 14:1 and Psalm 53:1 declare: "The fool says in his heart, 'There is no God.' "

Both versions of the parable stress the point that we, as individuals, are not self-sufficient. The rich fool, however, is not criticized because he is rich, but because he is a fool. In the Lucan version, which is more complete and original—and noting that the Egyptian editor may have changed Thomas 63 for reasons of his own—the fool died only after he had ceased the process of accumulation, and had made plans to eat and drink his stores. Had he been able to carry out his intentions, he would have become progressively less wealthy.

The man in the parable laid plans—and they were *his* plans solely. He thought to himself, "I will do this, and this." Nevertheless, he died and never got to do as he intended. Jesus meant that our function on earth is not to formulate our own plans, but to attune ourselves with God's. It is, further, our function to carry out his plans rather than act only from our limited intellect. When we receive divine ideas and work according to their potential, we become vehicles of God's creative energy and, in a valid sense, co-creators with God. This is success in the truest sense.

Luke's text, especially, takes issue with the view of Epicurus (342–270 B.C.). This Greek philosopher held that the primary purpose of life is to increase pleasure and to avoid pain. "Eat, drink, and be merry" expresses the essentials of his creed. This is a false attitude, because spiritual fulfillment can never come from earthly enjoyments.

Wholesome recreation is good for the soul and the body. Life is indeed for living. Nevertheless, the attitude of "eat, drink, and be merry" can reflect a depressed attitude as well as a positive one. There is a great difference between enjoying life because God is our life, and growing dissolute out of a feeling that life has lost its meaning.

Clement of Alexandria (150–220 A.D.) made the following points clear: A person can, by a low and mean choice, make pleasure the goal of life. There is, however, within us a basic, normal tendency to return to light, to God. This is part of our created being. It derives from God's nature, which is to give of his fullness to all. As Clement taught, true understanding is to see ourselves as participating in God, in Being itself. To know the indwelling Christ is the key to salvation or wholeness.

In summary, then, the parable of the rich fool focuses on the following points:

(1) We are dependent upon God for our being and continued existence.

(2) Our true function is not to make plans, but to implement those given to us by the universal intelligence.

(3) We are to look to our divine source for life, supply, and satisfaction. This encourages us to enjoy life, but rejects the "pleasure principle" as advocated by Epicurus.

Affirmations

I renounce the illusion of existence apart from God.

I rest in my eternal oneness with God.

The transforming power of divine love lifts me into a new realization of his abundant supply.

I am kept in perfect peace, for my mind is attuned to the God within.

I look to divine Mind as the source of all true ideas. The indwelling Spirit of God shows me the way.

I no longer expect satisfaction from outer things. I am satisfied by the infilling Spirit of God.

Chapter 31

The Children at Play

¹⁶"But to what shall I compare this generation? It is like children sitting in the market places and calling to their playmates,

¹⁷'We piped to you, and you did not dance;
we wailed, and you did not mourn.'

¹⁸For John came neither eating nor drinking, and they say, 'He has a demon'; ¹⁹the Son of Man came eating and drinking, and they say, 'Behold, a glutton and a drunkard, a friend of tax collectors and sinners!' Yet wisdom is justified by her deeds."
–*Matthew 11:16-19 (parallel passage: Luke 7:31-35)*

Both Jesus and John the Baptist are mentioned here, and the context is probably original. Both men refused to "play the games" of their generation. They were inner-directed, each with a God-inspired agenda of his own. Their critics, many of whom refused to even think in spiritual terms, ignored the substance of what they had to say. They rationalized this rejection by character attacking arguments against both, even though these complaints tended to contradict each other. They criticized John because he was ascetic, if not actually demon-possessed. At the same time, they criticized Jesus because he was *not* ascetic, and also kept bad company.

The brief parable in Matthew 11:16–17 portrays children shouting at each other. Some of them want to play at weddings and funerals, but others refuse. Playing the flute and dancing are customary at Near Eastern weddings, and it is the men who dance. Thus the players are boys. It is the women, however, who weep and wail at funerals. In this case, the players are girls.

Children of all generations have imitated adults, playing various roles. This is a normal part of childhood, and at times a charming one. Jesus, however, intended no compliment when he compared the men and women of his era to arguing boys and girls. He meant, rather, that the people of his time merely imitated life. They did not understand the laws of creative consciousness or the workings of their own minds. Thus, to use a modern proverb, they were "dead from the neck up." Their petty arguments and concerns had unfitted them for any higher purpose. They had rendered themselves unworthy of Jesus and his vision of the kingdom of God, self-condemned by their own mediocrity.

Paul may have had this parable in mind when he wrote: "When I was a child, I spoke like a child, I thought like a child, I reasoned like a child; when I became a man, I gave up childish ways"(1 Corinthians 13:11).

In addition, Jesus' intent may be discerned in *the form* as well as *the fact* of the game. The children played at weddings and funerals, i.e. at the apparent temporality of life. From a material point of view, human existence has its basics in birth, marriage, procreation, and death. From the standpoint of eternity, however, this is a masquerade. It is a passing show of merely transitory interest.

The I AM or cosmic Christ is without beginning and without end, and this is our true identity. Mystics of many religions have shared this realization, though they have expressed it in different terms. For example, the Isha Upanishad (Hindu) reads:

> To the illumined soul, the Self is all. For him who sees everywhere oneness, how can there be delusion or grief?
>
> The Self is everywhere. Bright is he, bodiless, without scar of imperfection, without bone, without flesh, pure, untouched by evil. The Seer, the Thinker, the One who is above all, the Self-Existent—he it is that has established perfect order among objects and beings from beginningless time.[1]

Jesus' uniqueness lies in the value he placed on earth life *as a proving ground for the use of spiritual laws.* A religion, to be adequate, must be spiritual *and* practical. Thus, in Matthew 11:19 we read, "wisdom is justified by her deeds." Or, as Origen quotes this proverb, "wisdom sends forth her children [i.e. results]."

The road to spiritual mastery, then, involves meeting challenges and overcoming them. To do so, *we need to examine our own thoughts, words, and motives to determine where they are leading us.* This, like the children in the parable, is what Jesus' adult critics failed to do. Had they done so, they would not have indulged in petty criticism. They would have shifted their attention from evil to good, from error to truth, from separation to oneness, from darkness to light, and in the process discovered their own divinity. This change of focus is still—and always will be—basic to a religion that works.

Affirmations

I awaken to Jesus' vision of the indwelling kingdom of God.

I am renewed and vitalized in and through the life that is God.

I accept my place of dominion within the divine order that is my heritage.

═══════════

Chapter 32

The Unfinished Tower/King's Warfare

> [28]"For which of you, desiring to build a tower, does not first sit down and count the cost, whether he has enough to complete it? [29]Otherwise, when he has laid a foundation, and is not able to finish, all who see it begin to mock him, [30]saying, 'This man began to build, and was not able to finish.' [31]Or what king, going to encounter another king in war, will not sit down first and take counsel whether he is able with ten thousand to meet him who comes against him with twenty thousand? [32]And if not, while the other is yet a great way off, he sends an embassy and asks terms of peace. [[33]So therefore, whoever of you does not renounce all that he has cannot be my disciple.]"   *—Luke 14:28–33*

These two parables fit together well, and there is no reason to doubt that Jesus gave them together. Nevertheless, verse 33 is out of context. It would fit well with the parables of the hidden treasure, the pearl, and the great fish, as commentary on the second step of the triad of *advent, reversal,* and *action.* Here, however, the theme is self-testing, not self-denial or the rejection of previously held beliefs. The tower-builder is not asked to abandon his project, but to consider whether or not he has the capital to complete it. The king does not abdicate his throne. He compares his own army with that of another king.

Towers were common in ancient Palestine. City-dwellers erected them to defend against military attack. Rural landowners also built them to guard their fields and vineyards. In the Old Testament, towers represent divine portection. for example:

> For thou art my refuge,
>   a strong tower against the enemy.   —Psalm 61:3

Jesus' parable, however, focuses on a different point. The man desires to build a tower, but it doesn't yet exist. What is more, the potential tower-builder considers whether or not he will build it. In so doing, he counts the cost. The king in the related parable also reviews the extent of his own resources before deciding what action to take.

Both parables relate spiritual consciousness to the achievement of specific goals. Jesus knew that wishing, in itself, does not make it so. Thought and imagery are primary and causal, but they must be applied in terms of energy and resources toward given goals. Many plans, including God-inspired ones, fail or never leave the drawing board, because of a lack of sustained vision and effort.

Ervin Seale, in his commentary, correctly points out that many people have stepped out on faith and achieved great things. It is necessary, however, to consider whether or not we have the consciousness to know that what is not yet visible is real. Without this awareness, we are liable to fall short of our goal. So the challenge suggested by the self-deliberations of the tower-builder and the king involves not only vision and effort, but also inner confidence and trust.[2]

In addition, the size of the armies in the second parable is significant. The king has ten thousand men in his army, and his rival has twenty thousand. This, in a numerological sense, contrasts *one* and *two*. *One* represents a realization of the unity of being, of one presence and one power. For the kingdom is a unitive state of consciousness, in which God is All-in-all. *Two*, by contrast, points to a belief in two contrary powers. The choice, then, is either to make the omnipresence of God the basis of thought, or to surrender to a false and dualistic belief system.

The image of truth attacking error has its limits. For what we attack we resist, and imbue with power. This is not an issue here, however, because *the rival king is the aggressor*. The king with ten thousand men is considering whether, as things stand, a defensive battle is worth the cost. So the parable's main theme is his two alternatives (which represent a choice that every individual must make). The king can either face the invading army of twenty thousand men, or arrange for his own surrender. There is no chance of a third choice, i.e. withdrawing from the field, for his rival has committed himself irrevocably. As with Julius Caesar, he has crossed the Rubicon River and "the die is cast."

Resolving to think according to oneness, as opposed to duality, is not strictly a war but it requires what Jimmy Carter called "the moral equivalent of war." It is not a hobby, or a pastime to be pursued casually in one's retirement. The contest is in the individual mind and heart. As such it is hard and subtle at times, but with God victory is certain. The real is always more powerful than the unreal, as a light that dispels the darkness.

Affirmations

Through Christ in me, I have the sustaining power to carry out every positive goal.

God is all, both invisible and visible.

One presence, one mind, one power is all.

This one that is all is perfect life, perfect love, and perfect substance.

Man is the individualized expression of God, and is ever one with this perfect life, perfect love, and perfect substance.

Chapter 33

The Barren Fig Tree

⁶And he told this parable: "A man had a fig tree planted in his vineyard; and he came seeking fruit on it and found none. ⁷And he said to the vinedresser, 'Lo, these three years I have come seeking fruit on this fig tree, and I find none. Cut it down; why should it use up the ground?' ⁸And he answered him, 'Let it alone, sir, this year also, till I dig about it and put on manure. ⁹And if it bears fruit next year, well and good; but if not, you can cut it down.' "

–Luke 13:6-9

According to tradition, the three years in the parable represent three years of Jesus' ministry. The barren fig tree is compared to the religious authorities in Jerusalem. Because of their rejection of Jesus and his message, they had failed to bear spiritual fruit. Yet at the time, there was still hope that they might change. It was a hope that, in retrospect, had failed. They approved the crucifixion of Jesus, and were themselves "cut down" with the fall of Jerusalem in 70 A.D.

This is a forced interpretation. It reflects Luke's preoccupation with the (then already past) overthrow of the sanhedrin and its allies. Far from dealing with concerns in Jerusalem, the parable reflects a rural setting. Jesus' hearers were peasant farmers, and the story's form reflects their interests. As in the parable of the wicked husbandmen, discussed in Chapter 22, the owner is an absent landlord who lives in the city. As a so-called gentleman farmer, *"he came seeking* fruit"(13:6).

It is also apparent that Jesus adapted this parable from a semitic folk tale. In this story, a son wishes to leave home and his father's employ. The father, however, considers him unready for this step and replies:

My son, you are like a tree which yielded no fruit, although it stood by the water, and its owner was forced to cut it down. And it said to him, Transplant me, and if even then I bear no fruit, cut me down. But its owner said to it, When you stood by the water you bore no fruit, how then will you bear fruit if you stand in another place?[3]

The country setting is evident, above all, by its use of manure as a metaphor. Manure is an earthy substance that a city man tends to regard as worthless. A farmer, however, values it highly because of its capacity to release growth in fruit-bearing trees and field crops. To him, it would be a fit symbol for the inner activity of Spirit. Midwestern farmers will say that Christ is in a manure pile without meaning any disrespect, but such a statement would not occur to a city dweller.

The central image of this parable is the fig tree. It grows in a vineyard, which is also of obvious importance since it points to the cultivated area of the mind. The tree is itself a symbol of the soul, especially in relation to inner growth of awareness. The image is archetypal, and is reflected in the Old Testament. For example, the book of Psalms begins:

> Blessed is the man
> who walks not in the counsel of the wicked,
> nor stands in the way of sinners,
> nor sits in the seat of scoffers;
> but his delight is in the law of the Lord,
> and on his law he meditates day and night.
> He is like a tree
> planted by streams of water,
> that yields its fruit in its season,
> and its leaf does not wither.
> In all that he does, he prospers.
> —Psalm 1:1–3 (cf. Jeremiah 17:7–8; Proverbs 3:18)

To the alchemists, the tree symbolized the uniting of man's visible body with his spiritual nature. Carl G. Jung and Mircea Eliade have independently verified this symbology through their research. Commenting on modern humanity, Dr. Jung concludes:

The alchemists saw the union of opposites under the symbol of the tree, and it is therefore not surprising that the unconscious of present-day man, who no longer feels at home in his world and can base his existence neither on the past that is no more nor on the future that is yet to be, should hark back to the symbol of the cosmic tree rooted in this world and growing up to heaven—the tree that is also man. In the history of symbols this tree is described as the way of life itself, a growing into that which eternally is and does not change; which springs from the union of opposites and, by its eternal presence, also makes that union possible.[4]

In addition, the *type* of tree that Jesus selected helps us to further define the parable's intent. The ancient Jews, including humble farmers, esteemed the fig tree both for its fruit and as a shade tree. It also represented freedom, peace, and prosperity.
For example, 1 Kings 4:25 reads:

And Judah and Israel dwelt in safety, from Dan even to Beer-sheba, every man under his vine and under his fig tree, all the days of Solomon (cf. 2 Kings 18:31; Isaiah 36:16; Joel 2:22; Micah 4:4; Haggai 2:19; Zechariah 3:10).

The fig tree, further, has an unusual trait. All trees of the genus *ficus* blossom within the fruit itself. "The minute flowers are aggregated within a pearlike or a globular fleshy receptacle called syconium...which has a small opening at the broad end."[5] It is therefore an especially fit symbol for the inner growth of awareness.
Yet in the parable, the tree is barren of any fruit. This represents the soul that is empty and fruitless in terms of spiritual progress. The tree, however, is not barren of hope. There is here a double numerical symbology that points toward possible fulfillment:
First, the tree had been expected to bear fruit for three years. The vinedresser appeals to the owner on the tree's behalf, asking that it be allowed to grow for a fourth year. This addition of a fourth member is significant because of the archetypal meaning of the number four. It is a symbol of wholeness.

In his study of psychological types, Jung stresses the basic nature of humanity as intuitive, emotional, mental, and physical. This agrees closely with the metaphysical tetrad of Spirit, soul, mind, and body.

Second, there is also an implied transition from six to seven. A tree was not expected to bear fruit during its first three years. Leviticus 19:23–25 reads:

> When you come into the land and plant all kinds of trees for food, then you shall count their fruit as forbidden; for three years it shall be forbidden to you, it must not be eaten. And in the fourth year all their fruit shall be holy, an offering of praise to the Lord. But in the fifth year you may eat of their fruit, that they may yield more richly for you: I am the Lord your God.

Three years of initial growth, added to three years of expected fruitage, equals six. Seven (6+1) is a symbol of fulfillment and completion. As God is said in the biblical allegory to have worked six days to create the earth, so the six days point to our own efforts toward spiritual growth. The number seven, which of course follows six, represents inner peace and fullness following a completed cycle of activity.

The parable of the barren fig tree thus presents a message of hope and promise. The nutrients are in the soil, waiting to be tapped. They may be "locked up," so to speak, but digging around the tree and adding manure will unlock that potential. So does the activity of God, when we are willing, release our spiritual potential into conscious expression as greater life, love, wisdom, and peace. When this occurs inwardly, we bear abundant fruit.

Affirmations

The activity of the Spirit within releases my true potential in and through me.

Through the Spirit of God in me, I can begin again. I am born anew into the infinite kingdom of God.

I experience the God within as life, love, wisdom, and peace.

Chapter 34

The Two Sons

[28]"What do you think? A man had two sons; and he went
to the first and said, 'Son, go and work in the vineyard
today.' [29]And he answered, 'I will not'; but afterward he
repented and went. [30]And he went to the second and said
the same; and he answered, 'I go, sir,' but did not go.
[31]Which of the two did the will of his father?" They said,
"The first."

Jesus said to them, "Truly, I say to you, the tax collectors and the harlots go into the kingdom of God before
you. [[32]For John came to you in the way of righteousness,
and you did not believe him, but the tax collectors and
the harlots believed him; and even when you saw it, you
did not afterward repent and believe him.]"

–Matthew 21:28-32

The gospel of Matthew places this parable in Jerusalem, a
context that can be accepted. The religious authorities there
were like the son who agreed to go into his father's vineyard,
but did not go. By contrast, many of the disgraced members of
society were like the son who first refused to go, but later went
and did his work. By asking his hearers which son did his
father's will, Jesus lured them into unwittingly passing judgment
on themselves.

Matthew 21:32, however, is redundant, adding nothing
essential to Jesus' point. More important, Luke 7:29-30 gives
the same basic data as Matthew 21:32, regarding John the
Baptist and the public's response to his work. Yet Luke does not
attribute this reference to Jesus, nor does he mention the parable in Matthew 12:28-30 at all. In addition, the parable's focus
is neither on John nor on any other historical leader. It gives

attention to the two sons and their change of heart. For these reasons, verse 32 is clearly a later addition to the scene.

In the parable, Jesus again uses the vineyard as a symbol of our consciousness and how we use it. Since we are made in the image of God who is divine Mind, the true work of a son of God is with the formative power of thought. Elizabeth Boyden Howes correctly observes:

> The vineyard produces grapes which produce wine, one of the great symbols of the spirit of transformation. The vineyard, symbolically and in reality, does not develop and grow of itself; it needs human help. Therein lies the significance of the cooperative effort required between the divine and the human.[6]

When our focus is only on the surface appearances of life, a formal piety will not help us. Rather, it can destroy us if we fancy that we are following God's rules, whereas in fact we are not. The creative law does not grant an exemption to the formally pious if they indulge in negative thinking. They have to suffer the consequences, the same as everyone else. On the other hand, if we fully practice constructive thinking, and also act according to our positive focus, we are fulfilling the work that the Father has sent us to do. If we sow good seed, we also reap a good harvest. No matter how bad our past may have been, morally or otherwise, we can then grow above and beyond it.

Words are exceedingly cheap. Many people read about mental and spiritual laws, and discuss them fluently, but do not apply them to any constructive purpose. They are like the son who agrees to go to the vineyard, but fails to do so. On the other hand, many have disgraced themselves in the past, but have since turned to God with the humility of little children. They are ready to be taught, and to use whatever faith and wisdom they already have. They are like the son who says he will not go, but later decides to get to work in the vineyard.

The end of self-deceit, and the beginning of real progress, is when we discern the difference between just talking and working actively with spiritual principles. As James 1:22 warns:

"Be doers of the word, and not hearers only, deceiving yourselves."

Affirmations

I am willing to give up all self-deception.

I am willing to be taught directly from the God within.

I abide in the divine Word, the indwelling Christ. I am a
doer of the Word in thought and in action.

Chapter 35

The Importunate Widow

> ¹And he told them a parable, to the effect that they ought always to pray and not lose heart. ²He said, "In a certain city there was a judge who neither feared God nor regarded man; ³and there was a widow in that city who kept coming to him and saying, 'Vindicate me against my adversary.' ⁴For a while he refused; but afterward he said to himself, 'Though I neither fear God nor regard man, ⁵yet because this widow bothers me, I will vindicate her, or she will wear me out by her continual coming.' " ⁶And the Lord said, "Hear what the unrighteous judge says. ⁷And will not God vindicate his elect, who cry to him day and night? Will he delay long over them? ⁸I tell you, he will vindicate them speedily. [Nevertheless, when the Son of man comes, will he find faith on earth?]"
>
> *–Luke 18:1–8*

Many persons born with good talents, recipients of splendid education, surrounded by numerous opportunities, still find themselves useless, worth little to themselves or others. What is their missing ingredient? The answer is found in the parable of the importunate widow, who portrays the trait of persistence.

Webster's New Collegiate Dictionary defines *importunate* as "troublesomely urgent." The American Heritage Dictionary reads, "stubbornly or unreasonably persistent in request or demand." While importunate is not a common adjective, it describes the attitude and actions of the widow in the parable.

In Luke 18:3, the King James Version has the widow demand, "*Avenge* me of mine adversary." Given the content of the parable, however, *vindicate* (used in the RSV) is the preferred translation of the Greek verb *ekdikeō*. She sought equity, not revenge. She needed to collect on a debt or other obligation validly owed to her husband's estate.

A second issue involves the final statement: "Nevertheless, when the Son of man comes, will he find faith on earth?" It would, if taken as genuine, imply that God the Father (represented by the crooked judge) is preventing Jesus' return to earth in glory, but the church (represented by the widow) should nevertheless beg for his return. If Christians keep on pleading vociferously, the Father will finally get tired of the noise and let the Son of man come back, who will then right all wrongs. This picture, however, is contrary to the substance of Jesus' parables and tends to obscure the meaning of the text we are considering. Therefore, we can reject it as a later interpolation.

The judge "neither feared God nor regarded man"(18:2). This is not strange, since in the traditional Near East judges were looked upon with suspicion and dread. They received no salary. Therefore, unless they were independently wealthy, they depended upon bribes from the well-to-do for their living. They did not want to accept cases brought by poor people or widows who had nothing to give them. The judge in the parable upheld the plaintiff's rights only because she was importunate, making a pest of herself in demanding justice.

This is also true to life in the sense that people sometimes get their way by demanding attention loudly and often. There is something to the saying that "the squeaky wheel gets the grease." It is not the most mature method for getting things done, but it works in given cases.

The parable thus teaches that *persistence brings results.* Church tradition is not entirely false in interpreting it as a call to persistence in prayer. The failure of tradition lies in its inadequate concepts about prayer. Jesus did not recommend begging and beseeching, or something that is engaged in only at set times and places. Rather, he taught a constant attitude of mind and heart. As Jesus declares in John 8:31–32:

> If you *continue* in my word [*Logos*, indwelling Christ], you are truly my disciples, and you will know the truth, and the truth will make you free.

Nor is true prayer loud and demanding:

"When you pray, go into your room and shut the door and pray to your Father who is in secret; and your Father who sees in secret will reward you" (Matthew 6:6).

Also, Jesus does not compare the unjust judge to God. In fact, he forms a striking contrast between them, declaring that "He [God] will vindicate them speedily"(18:8). That is to say, if even such a character as this judge will render a just decision, how much more will our divine Father-Mother meet our needs!

In fact, God has given us everything even before we ask. *Our part is to persist in claiming the health, wisdom, supply, and harmony that are our divine birthright.* We do this not to change God, but to remove our own stubborn resistance to the activity of Spirit in and through us.

Every sustained thought is a prayer, and is prophetic of future action and circumstance. Jesus had a realistic, rather than sentimental, view of the kingdom. He knew that the kingdom of God will not be realized on earth until the individual silences the babel in his own brain, and comes in tune with infinite Mind. He also gave the assurance, however, that "*If* you abide in me, and my words abide in you, ask whatever you will, and it shall be done for you" (John 15:7).

Affirmations

I persist in claiming my divine birthright of health, wisdom, supply, and harmony.

I persist in setting aside my own resistance to the activity of Spirit in and through me.

I persist in accepting the good that Spirit has already given me in lavish abundance.

=======

Chapter 36

The Importunate Friend

⁵And he said to them, "Which of you who has a friend will go to him at midnight and say to him, 'Friend, lend me three loaves; ⁶for a friend of mine has arrived on a journey, and I have nothing to set before him'; ⁷and he will answer from within, 'Do not bother me; the door is now shut, and my children are with me in bed; I cannot get up and give you anything'? ⁸I tell you, though he will not get up and give him anything because he is his friend, yet because of his importunity he will rise and give him whatever he needs."

–Luke 11:5–8

Luke 11:1–13 deals with effective prayer and the givingness of God. Verses 2–4 roughly parallel Matthew 6:9–13, and verses 9–13 resemble Matthew 7:7–11. Jesus presents these teachings, as usual, with vivid imagery and great insight. The question of original context, however, is not a major one in this case. The parable in 11:5–8 stands on its own merits, and we will treat it as a unit complete in itself.

In considering the setting for Luke 11:5–8, we should remember that the Near Eastern rules of hospitality carry great weight. They require that when even a stranger knocks on your door, you will feed him and admit him for the night. This is in the public interest, making it possible for most people to travel cheaply with relative safety. In this parable, the imperative is even stronger. A *friend* appears, and there is no food in the house. The host therefore has a sense of urgency—he *must* get bread to feed his friend. To fail in this would result in public humiliation and disgrace. Thus, he could not take "no" for an answer.

There is a touch of humor with the man who had gone to bed for the night. To grant the request, he would end up waking his children who slept with him, which was not an unusual arrangement in crowded living conditions. With all the excitement, it would be difficult to get them back to sleep, and he and his wife would have to sit up with them.

Despite the complaint in Luke 11:7, however, there is no serious doubt that he will lend the requester the three loaves. *The parable, being in the form of a rhetorical question, implies this certainty of outcome.* And, as with the importunate widow in Luke 18:2–5, the parable teaches that persistence brings results. Again, the implicit contrast between the reluctant friend and our willing God is sharp. There is also the added element of urgency. The widow could stand to wait a few more days, but the man in Luke 11:5–8 needs the three loaves, and he needs them now. What is more, he gets them.

This implies that God has ways and means we do not know to fulfill our most urgent needs. Many of the greatest healings have come forth, the most unlikely rescues have been made, and the most pressing financial needs have been met in unexpected ways, for one who has yielded himself or herself to God. The point is to keep on trusting God, and to maintain our connection with the one Mind, no matter what the temporary appearance may be.

Affirmations

I rejoice in the all-sufficient supply of my Father-Mother God.

I trust in the reliable nature of spiritual laws.

Through the awareness of the divine presence, I have all-sufficiency in all things.

Section VII—
THE CONSUMMATION

Jesus' primary concern is indeed the Kingdom but I would consider it equally clear that his is a very special understanding of this eschatological Kingdom, one which is, among other things, totally anti-apocalyptic.... Jesus' kingdom is a permanent possibility and not an imminent certainty.[1]

—John D. Crossan

It remains a fact worth pondering that Jesus had preached the kingdom, while the church preached Jesus. And thus we are faced with a danger: we may so preach Jesus that we lose the vision of the kingdom, the mended creation.[2]

—Krister Stendahl

The gospel of John affirms that eternal life is here, and that a transformed consciousness is already moving powerfully into human awareness. The gospel of Thomas, rediscovered in 1945, supports this affirmation. In the synoptic gospels, however, we find that many early Christians could not bear the full force of Jesus' parables. As a result—though probably with good intentions—many parables were misread and placed into a forced setting, which did more to conceal than to reveal their true significance.

The authors of Matthew, Mark, and Luke deserve our everlasting gratitude. Among other achievements, they preserved many of the parables that would otherwise have been lost. Nevertheless, then as now, it is a vain, and indeed a self-contradictory, hope that Jesus will reappear with a legion of angels and compel people to be peaceful. The entire trend of the para-

bles, in their original form, rejects the notion of a forced solution to the human condition. Instead, the in-breaking of the
kingdom always follows the basic law of creative consciousness:
as within, so without. Jesus' use of the parable form, in and of
itself, affirms this basic truth.

God's creative work is already complete in principle. It is
not, however, yet complete to individual awareness. In this
sense, a new age—in the original, biblical sense of the term—is
still to be consummated on earth. We can bring that finality
closer by determining to see things right, according to the "single eye" that beholds one presence, one mind, one power above
all, through all, and in all.

===

Chapter 37

The Fish Net

47"Again, the kingdom of heaven is like a net which was thrown into the sea and gathered fish of every kind; 48when it was full, men drew it ashore and sat down and sorted the good into vessels but threw away the bad. [49So it will be at the close of the age. The angels will come out and separate the evil from the righteous, 50and throw them into the furnace of fire; there men will weep and gnash their teeth.]"

—Matthew 13:47–50

Jesus here used the datival introduction. It is the case with the kingdom of heaven as with the narrative's end result, which is keeping the good fish and throwing away the bad.

Verses 49 and 50, however, are a later addition and should be disregarded. They reflect the author of Matthew's practice of making allegorical interpretations of Jesus' parables. We saw this also in Chapters 5 and 7 regarding the parable of the sower and the parable of the wheat and the tares. He adapted his commentary on the sower (Matthew 13:18–23) from that in Mark 4:14–20. The statements found in Matthew 13:37–43 (re the wheat and the tares) and in Matthew 13:49–50 are not, of course, from Mark. They are probably the Matthean author's own invention.

Jesus, then, did not have angels in mind when he spoke of the men who drew the fish ashore. Nor did he equate the fish with human beings as such. It is true that the men in the parable place the good fish in vessels, and throw the bad away. This, however, points to the simple fact that each individual needs to sort his or her own thoughts, ideas, habits, beliefs, and emotional patterns. The challenge is to keep what is good and worthy, and to get rid of what is negative and unworthy.

The *sea* is a symbol of the subconscious mind, both individually and collectively. Fish are abundant, yet below the surface. This is like the abundant images that are outside the threshold of conscious mind. Carl G. Jung noted: "The sea is the favorite symbol for the unconscious, the mother of all that lives."[3]

The *net* is the conscious phase of mind. A fisherman who casts his net into the water hauls in fish of many sizes, types, and qualities. This is analogous to what occurs when the conscious mind makes contact with the subconscious. The images that emerge into awareness vary greatly in their nature and quality.

Fishermen have to sort their catch. If a person fishes for food, the obvious choice is between those that are edible and those that are not. A commercial fisherman may keep some fish that are unfit for human consumption; they may be salable as fertilizer or for some other purpose. Jewish fishermen, however, also had to consider the difference between ceremonially clean and unclean fish. This adds force to the image of sorting in Matthew 13:48. Leviticus 11:9–12 reads:

> These you may eat, of all that are in the waters. Everything in the waters that has fins and scales, whether in the seas or in the rivers, you may eat. But anything in the seas or the rivers that has not fins and scales, of the swarming creatures in the waters and of the living creatures that are in the waters, is an abomination to you. They shall remain an abomination to you; of their flesh you shall not eat, and their carcasses you shall have in abomination. Everything in the waters that has not fins and scales is an abomination to you.

In Chapter 16, we put forth Philippians 4:8 as a guide for the selection process. Even with this guide, however, the difference between "good" and "bad" will not be clear in every case. The distinction can become blurred between (1) the promptings of the Holy Spirit on a superconscious level, and (2) conditioned responses centered in the subconscious phase of mind. If one is having difficulty, the correct approach is to go into meditation and then affirm divine guidance and right action. As Jesus taught: "The Counselor, the Holy Spirit, whom the Father will send in my name, he will teach you all things"(John 14:26).

The cleansing of the subconscious mind, however, has a twofold effect. When we sort our thoughts, as the fishermen in the parable sort their catch, we are also doing a valuable work for the whole human race. The more we focus on spiritual love, health, confidence, and wisdom, the more we dissolve hate, disease, fear, and ignorance. This applies not only to our own psyches, but to the collective consciousness of the planet. It hastens the final dissolution of evil appearances, and the consummation of the divine order.

There are two collectivities to be considered. One is the collective belief system already mentioned. It has a mixture of truth and error, of both positive and negative elements. The other, the dominant one—when we are aware of its dominance— is the realm of infinite ideas in which we live, move, and have our being. Divine Mind is always perfect and harmonious. The more we are attuned to Spirit, the more we share its dominion in an active and conscious way on earth.

Affirmations

I give my full attention to the God within.

Divine love, health, confidence, and wisdom now have their full and free expression through my soul and body.

Divine ideas are fully dominant within me. Any contrary beliefs and images are dissolved into their native nothingness, through the power of the indwelling Christ.

I affirm, and receive, divine guidance on this issue. I affirm, and perceive, right action as it applies to my life and affairs.

Chapter 38

The Man with the Sword

**Jesus said, "The kingdom of the father is like a certain
man who wanted to kill a powerful man. In his own house
he drew his sword and stuck it into the wall in order to
find out whether his hand could carry through. Then he
slew the powerful man."** *—Thomas 98*

This parable was lost until its rediscovery in the 1940s, and
is still virtually unknown. Its intent can be derived from its
images and symbols, and how they are related to each other.
Jesus again used the datival introduction, so the analogy focuses on the end result of the attacker's actions.

While there is no biblical parallel, some early Christians
knew of the parable. The Valentinian *Gospel of Truth* (approximately 150 A.D.) refers both to the jar (Thomas 97) and to the
sword (Thomas 98), and in the same order. That is to say, both
documents link the two parables together. The author of the
Gospel of Truth probably borrowed from the gospel of Thomas,
which was much earlier.

In Chapter 10, we noted that the *Gospel of Truth* freely
adapts the image of the jar. It mentions the sword, however, in
the same basic sense as in Thomas 98, Hebrews 4:12, and
Ephesians 6:17, referring to the Word of God:

A drawn sword of two edges cutting this way and that:
when came into the midst the Word who is in the heart of
those who speak it.[4]

The symbol of the *powerful man* or *strong man* also appears
in Matthew 12:29, Mark 3:27, Luke 11:21–22, and Thomas 35.
Mark 3:27 reads:

> No one can enter a strong man's house and plunder his
> goods, unless he first binds the strong man; then indeed he
> may plunder his house.

The strong man has usually been taken to represent Satan,
in the sense of a fallen angel who competes with God to control
the earth and its people. In this parable, however, the attacker
does not stop at tying up his enemy and plundering his goods.
He slays him with a sword. This contradicts the traditional view,
which holds that even a *fallen* angel is immortal.

If, instead, we take the strong man as a symbol of collective
error, he accords well with the parable. What he represents is
mortal. In the light of divine reality, the collective error is illusory and has only that existence which we temporarily give it by
our own beliefs. Charles Fillmore explained:

> The human race has formed laws of physical birth and
> death, laws of sickness and physical inability, laws making
> food the source of bodily existence, laws of mind that rec-
> ognize no other source of existence except the physical.
> The sum total of these laws forms a race consciousness sep-
> arate from and independent of creative Mind. When cre-
> ative Mind sought to help men spiritually, the mind of the
> flesh opposed it and made every effort to solve its prob-
> lems in its own way. The great need of the human family is
> mind control. Jesus showed us that mastery is attained
> through realization of the power of Spirit.[5]

The sword represents just this power of Spirit. The image
of iron (and its derivative, steel) has deep archetypal roots. Our
remote ancestors viewed it as a protection against every sort of
evil influence.[6] In the form of a sword, it also becomes an
offensive weapon in a symbolic sense, an instrument of spiritual
power. In the New Testament, it is an image of the *Logos*, or
word of truth, slaying what is false and negative in thought and
belief. For example, Hebrews 4:12 declares:

> For the word [*logos*] of God is living and active, sharper
> than any two-edged sword, piercing to the division of soul

and spirit, of joints and marrow, and discerning the thoughts and intentions of the heart.

Paul, in his allegory of the spiritual warrior, used the term *rhēma* (voice). This refers to the visible power and expression of the *Logos*:

> And take the helmet of salvation, and the sword of the Spirit, which is the word [*rhēma*] of God (Ephesians 6:17).

Returning to the parable itself, we find it describes a two-step strategy. The man first tests his own strength by running the sword into the wall of his own house. Only after doing so does he go out with his weapon and kill the strong man.

The hand is a symbol of executive power. It represents the power to extend thoughts and images into visible form. *The house* refers to one's individual consciousness. Jesus meant that we should first test the authority of the I AM or Word *with respect to our own mind, body, and affairs*. The man in the parable is *inside* his house when he rams the sword in and through the wall. This implies that the nature of the thrust is to penetrate from within outward: from Spirit (the sword), through soul (the house), and then into the body and outer conditions.

Having gained confidence and experience, the second step is to give attention to dissolving adverse thought *on a planetary basis*. We can do this by continuing to contemplate God as the one presence, one mind, one power, all-in-all. We can also do so, and especially, by joining with others in affirming universal love, wisdom, liberty, justice, and peace. This meditative activity has borne fruit in the liberation of eastern Europe and other areas.

As Paul Ricoeur declares in his essay on *The Hermeneutics of Testimony*,[7] the New Testament dramatizes the issue as a cosmic trial between God and the prince of this world, between Christ the faithful witness and the father of lies. In so doing, it affirms the final victory of universal truth over collective illusion. Our parable, too, assures us that the time of the "strong man" will end. It can and will be destroyed, root and branch, through the invincible power of the Christ, the Word of God.

Affirmations

I rejoice that the sword of the Spirit, the indwelling Christ, dissolves all that is unlike itself.

I rejoice in the invincible action of the Word in mind, body, and affairs.

Let peace come forth in every mind.
Let Love flow forth from every heart.
Let forgiveness reign in every soul.
Let understanding be the common bond.
And now from the Light of the world,
the One Presence and Power of the Universe responds.
The Activity of God is healing and harmonizing Planet
    Earth.
Omnipotence is made manifest.
I am seeing the salvation of the planet before my very eyes,
as all false beliefs and error patterns are dissolved.
The sense of separation is no more; the healing has taken
    place,
and the world is restored to sanity.
This is the beginning of Peace on Earth and Good Will
    toward all,
as Love flows forth from every heart,
forgiveness reigns in every soul,
and all hearts and minds are one in perfect understanding.
It is done. And it is so.

—John Price

Chapter 39

The Wise and Foolish Builders

[24]"Every one then who hears these words of mine and does them will be like a wise man who built his house upon the rock; [25]and the rain fell, and the floods came, and the winds blew and beat upon that house, but it did not fall, because it had been founded on the rock. [26]And every one who hears these words of mine and does not do them will be like a foolish man who built his house upon the sand; [27]and the rain fell, and the floods came, and the winds blew and beat against that house, and it fell; and great was the fall of it."
   —Matthew 7:24-27(parallel passage: Luke 6:47-49)

When we compare the sermon on the mount (Matthew 5–7) with similar sayings in the gospels of Luke and of Thomas, we find that each gospel lists them in a different order. This makes it likely that Matthew 5–7 is a literary composite, combining many sources into an extended discourse. The parable in Matthew 7:24-27, with its two houses, is a fitting conclusion to this great collection. Again the emphasis is on being a doer of the word, not a hearer only. Doing, of course, means mastering the inner realms of thought as well as taking overt action. Our thoughts, images, and beliefs determine our actions.

When building a house, the first step is to select a firm foundation. In Palestine the weather is generally dry, but sometimes there are hard rains. Dry wadis then become raging torrents, giving rise to flash floods. A house built on a rock will withstand the wind and flooding. If the builder only scratched the surface, however, and built on sand, the house will not last long. One storm can easily topple it.

The contrast between *wise* and *foolish* repeats a basic motif of the parable of the ten virgins in Matthew 25:1–10. Here also, to be wise is to open oneself to a universal level of consciousness. To be foolish is to limit oneself to a narrow and superficial range of perception.

The wise man builds his house upon a *rock*, which is an image of what is stable and permanent. This means to build one's consciousness upon the rock of the indwelling Christ and its perfect ideas. In Jewish mysticism and also in medieval alchemy, it is the stone upon which the ineffable name is written, meaning our own immortal Self.[8]

Building on *sand* has the opposite meaning. Sand dunes shift with every wind, and therefore are a symbol of instability and change. The foolish man builds his consciousness on the shifting sands of faddism, sensory appearances, and outer conditions. He identifies not with his immortal Self, but with fleeting thoughts, sensations, and desires.

The rock is an archetypal symbol. It is prominent in the Old Testament,[9] and identified with the Christ in the New Testament. For example, 1 Corinthians 10:1–4 (KJV) reads:

> Moreover, brethren, I would not that ye should be ignorant, how that all our fathers were under the cloud, and all passed though the sea; And all were baptized unto Moses in the cloud and in the sea; And did all eat the same spiritual meat; And did all drink the same spiritual drink: for they drank of that spiritual Rock that followed them: *and that Rock was Christ.*

1 Peter 2:4–5a (also cited in Chapter 22) takes a further step, relating the Christ mind to our own awareness:

> Come to him, to that living stone, rejected by men but in God's sight chosen and precious; and like living stones be built into a spiritual house [consciousness].

While the symbology of the rock is clear and definite, that of the rain/floods/winds is surprisingly flexible and open-ended. In one sense, the rain/floods/winds represent negative thoughts, beliefs, and emotions that lead the soul astray. In meeting and overcoming these, we are to rely upon the unchangeable rock, not on external helps which can be withdrawn. Emmet Fox, in his commentary, mentions "the winds, and rains, and floods of error, of fear, and doubt, and self reproach." He also warns against depending upon the sands of "will power...so-called material security...the good-will of others ...our own personal resources."[10]

It is equally valid, however, to view these weather phenomena as symbols of the action of divine Mind upon the collective consciousness of the planet. In the semi-arid Near East, *rain* signifies blessings, not hardships. This is what Jesus meant when he said, "your Father...sends rain on the just and on the unjust" (Matthew 5:45). The *floods* also symbolize how the realization of divine reality will finally sweep away every image and psychic content unlike itself. A belief structure built on the Christ truth will endure; one built on "sand" will be hard put to resist the coming flood of spiritual awakening. According to Matthew 24:37–39 (cf. Luke 17:26–27), Jesus used the allegory of the great flood to illustrate the same basic point:

> As were the days of Noah, so will be the coming of the Son of man. For as in those days before the flood they were eating and drinking, marrying and giving in marriage, until the day when Noah entered the ark, and they did not know until the flood came and swept them all away, so will be the coming of the Son of man.

Isaiah 11:9 presents the following picture:

> They shall not hurt or destroy
> in all my holy mountain;
> for the earth shall be full
> of the knowledge of the Lord,
> as the waters cover the sea.

Isaiah 28:16–18, which combines the images of the stone and the flood, is even more dramatic. The New English Bible translates:

These then are the words of the Lord God:
Look, I am laying a stone in Zion, a block of granite,
a precious corner-stone for a firm foundation;
he who has faith shall not waver.
I will use justice as a plumb-line
and righteousness as a plummet;
hail shall sweep away your refuge of lies,
and flood-waters carry away your shelter.
Then your treaty with Death shall be annulled
and your pact with Sheol shall not stand;
the raging waters will sweep by,
and you will be like land swept by the flood.

Since the time of Moses, *Yahweh* has been a basic Hebrew name for God. *Yahweh* and *I AM* have the same etymological root, signifying the God within which is known by many names, including the Oversoul, the Word, Logos, and Christ. *Wind* also signifies God as Spirit. An Arabic word, similar to *Yahweh*, means "to blow as the wind." And in John 3:8, Jesus relates the metaphors of wind and spirit to the new birth:

The *wind* blows where it wills, and you hear the sound of it,
but you do not know whence it comes or whither it goes;
so it is with every one who is born of the *Spirit*.

Both the Aramaic and Greek texts use a play on words, not with a humorous intent but to make a point. In Aramaic, the word *rokha* or *rukha* means *spirit, wind,* or *breath*. In Greek, the term *pneuma* carries the same three meanings.

In summary, then, those who build their house (consciousness) upon the rock of the Christ truth can rejoice. The "refuge of lies," which limits one's conscious union with God, will be swept away, and the "treaty with death" annulled. We shall be made new within and without, and the divine vision shall be consummated on earth.

Affirmations

I AM the rock, the living Word. I AM the Christ.
I build my consciousness on the rock, the indwelling Christ.

I am one with divine life, truth, love, and harmony.

I am washed clean by the flood of spiritual consciousness that now fills my entire being.

The living Spirit of God now sweeps through my soul, establishing joy and peace.

Chapter 40

The Lamp

¹⁴"You are the light of the world. A city set on a hill cannot be hid. ¹⁵Nor do men light a lamp and put it under a bushel, but on a stand, and it gives light to all in the house. ¹⁶Let your light so shine before men, that they may see your good works and give glory to your Father who is in heaven."
—*Matthew 5:14-16 (parallel passages: Mark 4:21-22;*
Luke 8:16-17; 11:33; Thomas 32-33)

Painters through many ages have depicted the holiness of the saints as an aura of light about the head. Most of us will see this blessedness in others by the presence of godly character. In one of the most appealing of Jesus' parables, "you are the light of the world," he calls us to so live in love toward others, that our "light" may "shine."

Jesus evidently used the brief parable in Matthew 5:15 many times. The five existing versions differ somewhat, in part because he adapted it to refer to his hearers' living arrangements which varied from place to place. Incidentally, the candles mentioned in the King James Version are incorrect. People in those days lit their homes with small oil lamps, not candles.

To people familiar with the Near East, Matthew 5:15 suggests a setting where several families live in a large, square, one-story house. Each family has its own lamp, but sometimes a given family will run out of the oil they need. At such times, they depend on their neighbors for light. Most people are happy to share in this way; but if there has been a quarrel, a family may put up a shade to limit the light available to their neighbors. If they are angry enough, they may place a meal tub over their

191

lamp. In a short time, the flame uses up the oxygen and goes out entirely.

The images in Matthew 5:14–16 are powerful and open-ended. Individual readers will relate to them in view of their own situation and needs. However, some points stand out most vividly:

You are the light of the world (5:14a). We share Jesus' function to show forth the qualities of God. He also said: "I am the light of the world; he who follows me will not walk in darkness, but will have the light of life" (John 8:12). Each of us, then—not Jesus alone—is a vehicle for manifesting the inner light. We are all the light of the world, through the I AM or indwelling Christ which is our spiritual Self.

A city set on a hill cannot be hid (5:14b). When our consciousness (city) is grounded in the divine presence (hill or mountain), it cannot be hid but shines forth for all to see. As Carl G. Jung observed:

> The mountain means ascent, particularly the mystical, spiritual ascent to the heights, to the place of revelation where the spirit is present. This motif is so well known that there is no need to document it.[11]

Mountains and hills are thus an archetype of illumination. Since early times, they have been regarded as the dwelling places of deity. To give a few examples: Moses received the ten commandments on Mount Sinai. Solomon built his temple on Mount Zion. The Samaritans worshipped on Mount Gerizim. The Greeks believed that their gods lived on Mount Olympus. In Japan, Fujiyama means "sacred mountain." Even in modern California, Mount Shasta has become holy and mysterious for many people. Mountains are also of some importance in the New Testament. Jesus was transfigured on one mountain, gave a sermon on another, and ascended from a third.

Nor do men light a lamp and put it under a bushel, but on a stand, and it gives light to all in the house (5:15). The lamp also points to inward illumination. It symbolizes the divine presence, even as does the lampstand in the tabernacle. Edward F. Edinger notes:

The outer chamber of the tabernacle contained the table of "show bread," the altar of incense and the lampstand. (Exodus 40:22–27) The latter is an obvious reference to the divine nature of light (consciousness).[12]

We are called to be clear channels of God's action. If we refuse the call and hide the light, we will put it out in our experience. We increase our awareness by sharing, as a radiating center of life, truth, love, joy, and every positive quality.

Let your light so shine before men, that they may see your good works and give glory to your Father who is in heaven (5:16). This is followed in Matthew 6:1 by the teaching: "Beware of practicing your piety before men in order to be seen by them." The child of light, and the "hypocrite" within the meaning of Matthew 6:2, 5, both show a certain quality. *The motive in the two cases, however, is completely different.* The hypocrite, as representing an attitude of mind, views himself or herself as strictly separate. The goal is to perform in a given way to bring credit to oneself. The true disciple, however, becomes a clear channel of the Spirit in order to glorify God, whether this leads to popularity or not. Through the divine law of expression, which is that *like produces like,* he or she affirms oneness with God through thought and action.

In summary, then, Jesus used images of light to affirm the omnipresence of God, and to take this basic truth to its logical conclusion. He envisioned love and light not only in the being of God, and in his own divine Self, but also in the passing appearances of life on earth. As we do this, with respect to the people and things in our experience, we find that love and light also increase in ourselves and shine through us. In the process, we consciously *become* the light that dissolves the darkness, and the love which casts out fear. This makes us an integral part of the second coming, which is continually happening for those who are ready, and in which earth is transmuted into heaven.

Affirmations

I AM the light of the world.
I let the inner light shine through me in thought, feeling, and action.

I am a radiant channel for the flow of divine life, truth, love, joy, and peace.

I see others as radiant channels for the flow of divine life, truth, love, joy, and peace.

God is the one creative Mind, the one creative action, and the one perfect result. I am eternally one with this divine law of expression.

Chapter 41

The Prodigal Son

[11]And he said, "There was a man who had two sons; [12]and the younger of them said to his father, 'Father, give me the share of property that falls to me.' And he divided his living between them. [13]Not many days later, the younger son gathered all he had and took his journey into a far country, and there he squandered his property in loose living. [14]And when he had spent everything, a great famine arose in that country, and he began to be in want. [15]So he went and joined himself to one of the citizens of that country, who sent him into his fields to feed swine. [16]And he would gladly have fed on the pods that the swine ate; and no one gave him anything. [17]But when he came to himself he said, 'How many of my father's hired servants have bread enough and to spare, but I perish here with hunger! [18]I will arise and go to my father, and I will say to him, "Father, I have sinned against heaven and before you; [19]I am no longer worthy to be called your son; treat me as one of your hired servants."' [20]And he arose and came to his father. But while he was yet at a distance, his father saw him and had compassion, and ran and embraced him and kissed him. [21]And the son said to him, 'Father, I have sinned against heaven and before you; I am no longer worthy to be called your son.' [22]But the father said to his servants, 'Bring quickly the best robe, and put it on him; and put a ring on his hand, and shoes on his feet; [23]and bring the fatted calf and kill it, and let us eat and make merry; [24]for this my son was dead, and is alive again; he was lost, and is found.' And they began to make merry.

[25]"Now his elder son was in the field; and as he came and drew near to the house, he heard music and dancing. [26]And he called one of the servants and asked what this

195

meant. ²⁷And he said to him, 'Your brother has come, and
your father has killed the fatted calf, because he has
received him safe and sound.' ²⁸But he was angry and
refused to go in. His father came out and entreated him,
²⁹but he answered his father, 'Lo, these many years I have
served you, and I never disobeyed your command; yet you
never gave me a kid, that I might make merry with my
friends. ³⁰But when this son of yours came, who has
devoured your living with harlots, you killed for him the
fatted calf!' ³¹And he said to him, 'Son, you are always
with me, and all that is mine is yours. ³²It was fitting to
make merry and be glad, for this your brother was dead,
and is alive; he was lost, and is found.' "

–Luke 15:11–32

Jesus' parable is a literary masterpiece. Its imagery is striking and its message profound. It is, of course, a parable about
two brothers, one who went far away and the other who stayed
home. Before we begin our analysis of the parable we can
emphasize the remarkable nature of its message by understanding what might have been common behavior in those times.

An ancient work, *The Apocalypse of Sedrach*, includes the following parable:

> Tell me, what sort of a father would give an inheritance to
> his son, and having received the money the son goes away
> leaving his father, and becomes an alien and in the service
> of aliens. The father then, seeing that the son has forsaken
> him and gone away, darkens his heart and going away, he
> retrieves his wealth and banishes his son from his glory
> because he forsook his father.¹³

Jesus may have heard this story, and then given his parable
of the prodigal son partly in reaction to it. Both accounts begin
in a similar way, but depart fundamentally at a certain point. In
one, the father himself chases after the son and reclaims his
wealth. According to this picture, God rejected the human race,
taking back the glory and dominion that had once been our
heritage. In the other, the son first spends everything. Later, he
comes to himself, changes his thinking, and returns to his

father who welcomes him home, thus illustrating the love of a forgiving God.

We need not be concerned that the parable was too long for its original hearers to remember correctly. Many people of the Orient had, and still have, highly trained memories. They use mental picturing and other procedures that are just now being learned in the western world. It is entirely plausible for a trained listener to have remembered the parable of the prodigal son in its entirety. Jesus could have recorded it in writing, but this would not have been essential to preserve its original wording.

Turning then to Luke 15:11–24, we find a story of a young man who "sows his wild oats" and later reaps the results of his actions. He comes to see the error of his ways and returns home, where his father forgives him. The parable does not minimize the negative results of a dissolute life, nor is his youth any excuse. At the same time, the text is emphatic in saying that there is a way out. The father is a symbol of God, who reveals his nature through love, grace, and forgiveness.

The moral downfall and reform of the younger son, however, is only the parable's surface meaning. In a wider sense, it sums up the spiritual history of the human race. Forgetting God is part of the symbology. For as the German scholar, Günther Bornkamm, points out in his commentary, a son does not normally inherit from his father's estate until the father has died. So here we have an early example of the "God is dead" syndrome (15:12). The parable does not give details as to how humanity lost a consciousness of unity with God. It deals rather with the potentials of the present moment for awakening from spiritual sleep, and being restored to active, conscious oneness with the Father.

The younger son "took his journey into a far country" (15:13). This represents the human soul when it loses contact with the divine presence, and becomes engrossed in material appearances. The "far country" is not a place; it is a belief in external causes and manifold powers, and is foreign to the true understanding of life.

In this far country, the younger son "squandered his property in loose living." The King James Version reads that he "wasted his substance in riotous living." Outwardly this implies lust, drunkenness, and the squandering of money. Inwardly, it means that when the soul loses its awareness of God as the one presence and one power, it becomes prone to a riot of confusion. In such a chaotic state, one's mental substance is depleted and the realization of spiritual power is lost.

"And when he had spent everything, a great famine arose in that country, and he began to be in want" (15:14). A belief in separation from our spiritual source is certain to create feelings of lack and limitation. A negative series of consequences is set loose, and all seems empty and meaningless. A famine of good is experienced. At this point, however, a great yearning for lost peace and satisfaction may well up within. Out of a deep sense of lack, sorrow, and despair, hope reappears for a return to spiritual wholeness.

"So he went and joined himself to one of the citizens of that country, who sent him into his fields to feed swine" (15:15). To Jewish people, whom Jesus addressed here, the occupation of swineherd was more than unattractive. It represented the depths of degradation. The pig is a ceremonially unclean animal. Also, kosher food often was not available in foreign lands. This made travel more difficult for devout Jews.

"And he would gladly have fed on the pods that the swine ate; and no one gave him anything" (15:16). The pigs in question did not eat general slop. The text refers to the bean of the carob tree. There are, however, two varieties. The sweet kind is sometimes used today as a substitute for chocolate. The other kind is different, being bitter to the human taste. Jesus probably meant the bitter pods, emphasizing the bitterness of the fallen man's condition.

While in this low estate, the prodigal remembered that he was his father's son. *Nothing he did, or failed to do, could change this fact.* Likewise, we are eternal children of God, whether we know it or not, and whether or not our thoughts and actions reflect our true nature. Rising out of sorrow and emptiness of heart, *he came to himself* [in Greek, *eis heauton...elthōn*] (15:17).

That is, he began to realize his true self, the indwelling

Christ. This points to our need for spiritual reawakening. In the Greek text, the phrase means to awaken after having fainted or passed out. He "came to," as we would say in English. The *Gospel of Truth* 30:12–14 expresses the same idea in the form of a beatitude: "Blessed is the man who has returned to himself and awakened."

The prodigal determined to arise and return to his father (15:18). This represents the soul arising from its self-inflicted confusion to a realization of oneness with God. We all need to admit that we have fallen short of the life of a child of God. The soul must first perceive its mistakes, and then repent. Repentance is the first step back to *the Father's house*, which means the consciousness of divine Mind as the source of our being.

The meaning of repentance, however, is often misunderstood. It does not imply a continual burden of guilt, sorrow, and remorse. The New Testament term translated "repentance" is *metanoia*, which means "to change the mind; to change the inner man." This word, in turn, is derived from *meta* (beyond) and *nous* (the reasoning mind). In other words, repentance is illumination into a higher order of understanding, beyond left-brain reasoning and logic.

The father's actions at his son's return depict true forgiveness. "And he arose and came to his father. But while he was yet at a distance, his father saw him and had compassion, and ran and embraced him and kissed him" (15:20). There is no condemnation in the father's heart as he sees his son approaching. In fact, he does not respond to the son's confession of being a sinner—he changes the subject! Even the kiss is a symbol of forgiveness, as when King David kissed Absalom in 2 Samuel 14:33.

In addition, the father conferred the symbols of royalty and dominion upon his returning son. "Bring quickly the best robe, and put it on him; and put a ring on his hand, and shoes on his feet" (15:22). Apparently Jesus adapted this from Genesis 41:42, where Pharaoh makes Joseph second in command in Egypt.

> Then Pharaoh took his signet ring from his hand, and put
> it on Joseph's hand, and arrayed him in garments of fine
> linen.

Bring quickly the best robe, and put it on him. The best robe is
one of the primary symbols of royalty. Every person is meant to
be a king or queen over his or her own thinking, his or her
mental universe, in cooperation with divine Mind. The best
robe also refers to the consciousness of the unity of being. It is
the same as the new garment discussed in Chapters 4 and 15,
the vision of the universe in its spiritual oneness, whole and
complete in God.

Put a ring on his hand. The ring is a symbol of power. In
this context, it points to spiritual dominion and authority. To
this day, the reigning monarchs of England and other kingdoms
are given a ring, i.e. a signet ring which contains a royal seal or
imprint.

A ring also symbolizes infinity, being a circle, which is
without beginning and without end. In addition, in the parable
the ring is placed on the son's hand, rather than on his finger.
There is reason for this slight misstatement. The hand represents the power to demonstrate an idea, to bring inner ideas
into practical use and visible form. As examples, "the right
hand of God" and "the king's hand" are well-known symbols of
power.

According to Carl G. Jung, the circle stands for psychic
wholeness. It represents the Self, the archetypal symbol of the
indwelling Christ. As such it has many expressions, e.g. in
dreams, myths, the zodiac, architecture, and the mandalas that
derive from the Tibetan tradition.

And shoes on his feet. The shoes being placed on the son's
feet represent the bestowal of spiritual understanding. This
symbolic meaning is reflected, for example, in Psalm 119:105:

> Thy word is a lamp to my feet
> and a light to my path.

"And bring the fatted calf and kill it, and let us eat and
make merry" (15:23). The calf or bull, a primary archetypal

symbol, represents physical strength and fertility. In early days, the calf or bull was worshiped in connection with the rites of Baalism. The Egyptians worshiped Apis the bull, and the golden calf of the Israelites in the desert was of this kind.

In later centuries, the symbol lost its grosser connotations and came to be equated with health and healing. To eat the fatted calf is thus to assimilate—and thereby to transmute—the richness of mental, emotional, and physical vitality that are available in, and from, God as the life principle.

Making merry is here a symbol of the kingdom. It has none of the negative meaning of the parable of the rich fool (Luke 12:16–20). Rather, it expresses the joy of a restored Father-son relationship with God.

"For this my son was dead, and is alive again; he was lost, and is found" (15:24). Jesus here uses two analogies, that of rising from the dead, and of a shepherd finding his lost sheep (though a sheep is not specifically mentioned). The text repeats this statement in 15:32, as part of the father's answer to the protest of his older son. Jesus' listeners would have thought that 15:24 was the end of the parable. He continued, however, with 15:25–32.

The elder son was jealous and resentful of the special attention given to his brother. At first thought, most people would sympathize with the older son. He seems justified in looking down upon his younger brother who had acted so shamefully.

We need a true estimate of the elder son in order to accurately interpret his meaning. According to one view, the parable is a commentary on human evolution. The brother who stays home represents a merely instinctual level of the psyche, as with an animal. He does not err, but—having no conscious will—neither does he progress. The younger brother, by contrast, points to the development through which the soul becomes conscious of itself, i.e. human, and able to make choices. The latter makes many mistakes in the process, but at last unites consciously with God.

This view, however, is disharmonious with the text and must therefore be rejected. The elder brother, in the parable, is

at work "in the field" (15:25). The meaning here is agricultural;
he works with the land. This is the archetypal opposite of the
wilderness, which could symbolize the instinctual. In the Greek
text, the word for "field" is *agros*, reflected in the English term
agriculture. Agros means a field used to grow crops, never a wild
place.

Others have claimed that the elder son represents a merely
negative kind of righteousness. He stays out of trouble, but isn't
much good for anything. Still others believe that he reflects a
high spiritual outlook. He is holy, whereas his brother is unholy.
Instead of these speculations, *let us review how the parable actually reads,* noting that it is a literary skill to sometimes suggest—
rather than specifically state—a person's traits of character.
Viewing the text in this way, we find that he possesses certain
manly virtues. The fact that he is placed in the field (15:25)
implies that he is a hard and diligent worker. He told his father,
without fear of contradiction: "Lo, these many years I have served
you, and I never disobeyed your command" (15:29). Thus he
had been loyal at all times, and true to his word. The younger
brother, in stark contrast, saw that he had utterly failed to live
up to his father's standards, and lamented: "I am no longer worthy to be called your son" (15:19, 21).[14]

Emmet Fox declared that Jesus is the most revolutionary of
all teachers, and this parable supports his claim. The prodigal
son joins in the feast, which is held in his honor. The virtuous
older brother remains outside. The reversal is even stronger
here than in the good Samaritan (Luke 10:30–36), and the
Pharisee and the publican (Luke 18:9–14). For the priest, the
Levite, and the Pharisee were, in the last analysis, religious
freaks. The same cannot be said, however, about the loyal,
upright, hard-working elder son.

Jesus' use of the reversal theme highlights what the elder
son refused because of his attitude. Though indeed faithful and
industrious, he had missed the central purpose of life, which is
awakening to our conscious oneness with God. He was as dissociated from his true being as the prodigal had been while away
from home. He emerges as a symbol of the egocentric image of
self, which resents the supremacy of the Christ self and there-

fore avoids the messianic banquet. In fact, the attitudes that he portrays can cut one off from the joy and peace of the divine presence just as certainly as a life of dissipation and vice.

"And as he came and drew near to the house, he heard music and dancing" (15:25). The Father's house, as already noted, is the consciousness of divine Mind as the source of our being. Making merry points to the joy and abundance of the kingdom of God. In addition, the dance referred to here is *the round dance*. The word in the Greek text, *choros*, leaves no doubt as to its meaning. It applied to a group of people who sang and danced in a ring.

The round dance is a symbol of great importance. It has all the meanings of the ring or circle, and also represents the relation of each individual to the cosmic Christ. The apocryphal *Acts of John* includes a mystical round dance, in which the twelve apostles are depicted holding hands and dancing around Jesus, who stands in the center.,

Carl G. Jung discussed this symbology at length. He explained:

> Since olden times the circle with a centre has been a symbol for the Deity, illustrating the wholeness of God incarnate: the single point in the centre and the series of points constituting the circumference...the aim and effect of the solemn round dance is to impress upon the mind the image of the circle and the centre and the relation of each point along the periphery to that centre.[15]

We then become identified not with personal limitations, but with the Christ in us:

> When you relate to your own (transcendental) centre, you initiate a process of conscious development which leads to oneness and wholeness. You no longer see yourself as an isolated point on the periphery, but as the One in the centre.... Whoever joins in the dance sees himself in the reflecting centre.[16]

The celebration in the Father's house is thus to be contrasted with the forlorn stance of the elder brother. He complains that his brother gets the veal, but he doesn't even qualify for a meal of goat's meat: "You never gave me a kid, that I might make merry with my friends. But when this son of yours came, who has devoured your living with harlots, you killed for him the fatted calf!" (15:29–30). He doesn't even acknowledge that the ex-prodigal is his brother. In fact, he denounces him for wasting their father's own money on whores.

The father's answer to this complaint (15:31) expresses the essence of the kingdom. It points to the realization which, when widely held, will consummate God's glorious plan on earth.

Son, you are always with me. God is omnipresent. Therefore, his good—which is without an opposite—is here and now. We can never be separated from it. The kingdom is not a future hope or expectation, but is within us now to be discovered.

All that is mine is yours. God, the supreme mind and source of all, has made himself available to us, through right mental and spiritual attunement. The elder brother, had he accepted it, would not have had to earn his keep by the sweat of his brow. He could have had anything that the father had, at any time.

Both sons, despite the greatest variations in life-style, had a common lack: they had forgotten their true status in relation to their father and his resources. Similarly, whether your life has been more akin to that of the elder brother, or to that of the younger, the solution to the problems of life is basically the same. Begin to live with a new spirit, confident that God is omnipresent and available to meet your every need. And, in so doing, work with the one perfect Mind to dissolve the illusory thoughts, images, and beliefs that would negate this central truth.

As the English metaphysician F.L. Rawson superbly declared:

> The "end of the world" simply means the end of all false material mentality, all sin, sickness, worries, troubles, and limitations, literally their final disappearance.... In other words, we all wake up from this self-maintained dream, to find ourselves in an absolutely glorious world, in which we, the real beings, have always been and always shall be.[17]

Affirmations

With joy I return to the Father's house, the Christ consciousness.

I am taught, inspired, and empowered through the God within.

I am in the Father, and the Father is in me. The kingdom of God is within me, and within all people everywhere.

All that the Father has is mine. I receive the good that the Father has established from the foundation of the world.

Index of Jesus' Parables

Index of the Parables and Crossan's "Sayings Parallels: A Workbook for the Jesus Tradition"

Basic Bibliography

Roberto Assagioli, *Psychosynthesis*. Penguin Books, 1976.

William J. Bausch, *Storytelling: Imagination and Faith*. Twenty-Third Publications, 1984.

John Dominic Crossan, *In Parables–The Challenge of the Historical Jesus*. Harper & Row, Publishers, 1973.

____*Cliffs of Fall--Paradox and Polyvalence in the Parables of Jesus*. The Seabury Press, 1980.

Elizabeth Boyden Howes, *Jesus' Answer to God*. Guild for Psychological Studies Publishing House, 1984.

Joachim Jeremias, *The Parables of Jesus,* second revised edition. Charles Scribner's Sons, 1972.

Maurice Nicoll, *The New Man*. Vincent Stuart, 1950. Currently available from Shambhala Publications, Inc.

Norman Perrin, *Jesus and the Language of the Kingdom*. Fortress Press, 1976.

John A. Sanford, *The Kingdom Within*. Paulist Press, 1970.

Bernard Scott, *Jesus, Symbol-Maker for the Kingdom*. Fortress Press, 1981.

Ervin Seale, *Learn To Live*. William Morrow & Company, 1955. Currently available from Science of Mind Publications.

Dan O. Via Jr., *The Parables: Their Literary and Existential Dimension*. Fortress Press, 1967.

Walter Wink, *Transforming Bible Study*. Abingdon Press, 1980.

Chapter Summaries

1. *The Hidden Treasure*—The hidden treasure is the divine presence within. To claim this treasure is to realize our true identity which is one with God.

2. *The Pearl*—The pearl is also our true spiritual identity which is one with God. We have to "sell" limiting and demeaning ideas about ourselves in order to "buy" this pearl, and thus gain true confidence in life.

3. *The Great Fish*—Found only in the gospel of Thomas, rediscovered in 1945, this parable uses the great fish as a symbol of the indwelling Christ. The fisherman chooses to land this fish, and to throw back the smaller fish.

4. *The Cloth and Wineskins*—These twin parables refer to giving up old ways of viewing life, and gaining a new vision of the universe as whole and complete.

5. *The Sower*—The sower goes forth to sow, and the seeds fall on four types of ground. Different soils respond differently to the same type and quality of seed. In the same way, various people respond differently to the same spiritual ideas and teachings.

6. *The Seed Growing Secretly*—In this parable, the sower is like the conscious mind which sows seed-thoughts in the subconscious mind. The result is a harvest in our everyday lives.

7. *The Wheat and the Tares*—The wheat and the tares represent true ideas and error thoughts, and how they can be separated. We learn to deny, but not to resist, what is contrary to our divine nature.

8. *The Mustard Seed*—The mustard seed teaches that spiritual consciousness can begin very small among all the thoughts of the mind, and yet grow to become completely dominant.

9. *The Leaven*—The Spirit's action within the psyche is silent and invisible, yet powerful, like leaven's action in a loaf of bread. Yet the tangible results are plainly visible.

10. *The Jar*—A parable known only from the gospel of Thomas, it illustrates how the deeper vitality of our lives can be slowly lost through neglect.

11. *The Great Supper*—People give various excuses for not coming to the host's banquet. The table is set for us to receive God's supply of all that is good, but we have to want it in order to receive it.

12. *The Chief Seats*—There are two basic ways to make progress in life. One way is by striving and struggling in competition with other people. The other way, more effective in the long run, is to build a mental equivalent of what we want.

13. *The Ten Virgins*—Meditation and other spiritual disciplines are needed for us to enter the marriage feast of conscious oneness with God. The five wise girls in the parable were prepared, while the foolish five were not.

14. *The Rich Man and Lazarus*—Not an authentic parable of Jesus, it is based on an Egyptian folk tale. Yet it accords with the basic intuition that life is ultimately just, even where it seems unfair.

15. *The Wedding Robe*—The old garment symbolizes the old images of sin, disease, lack, and separation. The wedding garment represents the soul transformed through the realization of oneness with God, wherein we are whole and complete.

16. *The Doorkeeper*—We need to stand porter at the door of thought, to rise above fear and discouragement, and to dwell mentally on what is positive, peaceful, and whole.

17. *The Faithful Servants/Servant Entrusted with Supervision*—Every person is a steward. We are entrusted with the supervision of our thoughts, words, and beliefs, and thus we shape our own lives.

18. *The Talents*—Use is the law of increase. It is important in life to step out in faith and to take a risk; otherwise, we can lose even what we have.

19. *The Laborers in the Vineyard*—The boss pays the workers according to the agreement they made with him. In like man-

ner, a person is compensated according to the deal he or she makes with life.

20. *The Unprofitable Servant*—The unlimited power of God is already within, but we have to work with it constantly and faithfully in order to show forth its benefits.

21. *The Unrighteous Steward*—The children of light need to be as consistent in applying their own vision of reality, as the scoundrel is consistent in applying his own beliefs.

22. *The Wicked Husbandmen/Rejected Cornerstone*—To symbolically "kill" the son is to turn from the divine Self within, and thus to destroy one's own character. Yet there is a road back, a new frame of reference symbolized by the cornerstone.

23. *The Lost Sheep*—This parable has several layers of meaning. Among other meanings, God seeks us out to respond positively to the movement of his life, love, and wisdom within us.

24. *The Lost Coin*—Like the woman searching for the lost coin, we need to bring the light of healing into the dark house, the dark areas of the psyche. The result of doing so is joy, peace, and vitality.

25. *The Two Debtors*—The harlot was restored to the wholeness of life because of her ardor for Jesus' truth. She loved much, and was therefore forgiven much.

26. *The Unmerciful Servant*—We have to forgive in order to be forgiven. This includes forgiving others, forgiving and accepting oneself, and forgiving false and limiting beliefs of every kind.

27. *The Throne Claimant*—Hate and revenge produce more of the same. But love and good will also produce more of the same, and return to bless the individual.

28. *The Pharisee and the Publican*—This parable portrays two states of consciousness. One, that of the Pharisee, closes the door to forgiveness. The other, that of the publican, opens the door. The goal, however, is to advance beyond both of the attitudes portrayed in the parable, so as to realize wholeness.

29. *The Good Samaritan*—Another parable with several layers of meaning. As Crossan wrote: "The hearer struggling with the contradictory dualism of Good/Samaritan is actually experiencing in and through this the inbreaking of the Kingdom."

30. *The Rich Fool*—The character in the parable is refuted not because he is rich, but because he is a fool. In the biblical sense, a fool is one who does not believe in God, or who conducts his or her life as if this were so.

31. *The Children at Play*—Jesus' picture of children is usually positive, but this parable is an exception. It portrays arguing children as a parody of the petty arguments and concerns of adults.

32. *The Unfinished Tower/King's Warfare*—These twin parables teach that while thought is primary and causal, it must nevertheless be applied in terms of energy and resources toward given goals.

33. *The Barren Fig Tree*—The fig tree has an unusual trait, in that it blossoms within the fruit itself. This is an especially fit symbol for the inner growth of awareness.

34. *The Two Sons*—The end of self-deceit, and the beginning of real progress, is when we discern the difference between just talking, and working actively with spiritual laws—and then do it.

35. *The Importunate Widow*—Persistence brings results, as shown with the widow appealing to the unjust judge. We need to persist in claiming the health, wisdom, supply, and harmony that are our divine birthright—not to change God, but to overcome our own resistance to God's action in our lives.

36. *The Importunate Friend*—God has ways and means we do not know, to fulfill our most urgent needs. The man in the parable needed three loaves of bread immediately, and he got them.

37. *The Fish Net*—As the men in the parable sorted their catch of fish, we need to sort our thoughts, ideas, habits, beliefs, and emotional patterns, keeping the positive and getting rid of the negative.

38. *The Man with the Sword*—This parable is found only in the gospel of Thomas. The hero slays the villain of collective error, which can and will be ultimately destroyed, root and branch, through the living Word of God.

39. *The Wise and Foolish Builders*—The wise man in the parable built his house upon a rock, symbolizing the cosmic

Christ and its perfect ideas. The foolish man built his house on sand, meaning faddism, sensory appearances, and outer conditions.

40. *The Lamp*—If we hide our inner light, we put it out of our experience. If we let the light shine through us, we increase our awareness by sharing, as a radiating center of life, truth, love, and joy.

41. *The Prodigal Son*—The prodigal son had some hard lessons to learn, but so did his elder brother. At the parable's end, the prodigal enters his father's house while the elder brother remains outside. What does this mean? Read the chapter and find out.

Notes

INTRODUCTION

1. Joseph Campbell with Bill Moyers, *The Power of Myth*. New York: Doubleday, 1988, p. 71.
2. Dolores Krieger, *The Therapeutic Touch: How to Use Your Hands to Help or to Heal*. Englewood Cliffs: Prentice-Hall, 1979, p. 78.
3. Norman Perrin, *Jesus and the Language of the Kingdom*. Philadelphia: Fortress Press, 1976, p. 3.
4. Carl G. Jung, *The Archetypes and the Collective Unconscious*. Princeton: Princeton University Press, 1959, pp. 3–4.
5. William Barclay, *Introducing the Bible*. Nashville: Abingdon Press, 1972, p. 129. Emphasis is Barclay's.
6. Ira Progoff, *The Symbolic and the Real*. New York: The Julian Press, Inc., 1963, p. 200.

SECTION I—THE REVOLUTION WITHIN

1. Carl G. Jung, *Aion–Researches into the Phenomenology of the Self*. Princeton: Princeton University Press, 1959, p. 221.
2. John Dominic Crossan, *In Parables–The Challenge of the Historical Jesus*. New York: Harper & Row, Publishers, 1973, p. 34.
3. Elizabeth Boyden Howes, *Jesus' Answer to God*. San Francisco: Guild for Psychological Studies Publishing House, 1984, p. 88.
4. James M. Robinson, ed., *The Nag Hammadi Library*. San

Francisco: Harper & Row, Publishers, 1977, p. 137. Translated by Wesley W. Isenberg.

5. *Aion,* pp. 72–172.
6. Jesus often used this saying. It is found in Matthew 11:15; 13:9, 43; Mark 4:9, 23; 7:16; Luke 8:8; 14:35; Thomas 8, 21, 24, 63, 65, 96.
7. Ervin Seale, *Learn To Live.* New York: William Morrow & Company, 1955, p. 137.
8. Robert Winterhalter, *The Odes of Solomon: Original Christianity Revealed.* St. Paul: Llewellyn Publications, 1985, p. 62. Translation by James H. Charlesworth.

SECTION II–SOWING AND REAPING

1. Walter Wink, *The Bible in Human Transformation.* Philadelphia: Fortress Press, 1973, p. 27.
2. *Jesus and the Language of the Kingdom,* p. 143. Emphasis is Perrin's.
3. Charles C. Torrey, *Our Translated Gospels.* New York: Harper & Brothers, 1936, p. 8. Emphasis is Torrey's.
4. Emmet Fox, *The Sermon on the Mount.* New York: Harper & Brothers, 1934, pp. 86–87. Emphasis is Emmet Fox's.
5. *The Archetypes and the Collective Unconscious,* p. 382.
6. *Learn To Live,* pp. 87–88.
7. Kendrick Grobel, *The Gospel of Truth,* Nashville: Abingdon Press, 1960, pp. 168, 170.

SECTION III–THE BANQUET PARABLES

1. S. I. Hayakawa, *Language in Thought and Action,* San Diego: Harcourt, Brace and World, Inc., 1940, p. 25.
2. *The Archetypes and the Collective Unconscious,* p. 243.
3. *Ibid.,* pp. 233–234.
4. Joachim Jeremias, *The Parables of Jesus,* second revised edition. New York: Charles Scribner's Sons, 1972, p. 64.
5. George Lamsa, *Gospel Light,* revised edition. Philadelphia: A.J. Holman Company, 1939, p. 273.

6. *Jesus' Answer to God,* p. 91.

7. *The Parables of Jesus,* pp. 171-174.

8. *Gospel Light,* p. 137.

9. For a further discussion of the sacred marriage motif, see Gerald H. Slusser's book, *From Jung to Jesus,* published by John Knox Press, esp. Chapter IX, "The Sacred Marriage of the Hero."

10. *The Parables of Jesus,* p. 183.

11. George Lamsa, *My Neighbor Jesus.* New York: Harper & Row, Publishers, 1932, p. 65.

12. For two twentieth century interpretations of the rich man and Lazarus, see Charles Fillmore, *Talks on Truth,* revised edition. Lee's Summit: Unity Books, 1934, pp. 146–160, and John Sanford, *The Kingdom Within.* New York: Paulist Press, 1970, pp. 176–178.

13. *The Parables of Jesus*, pp. 68–69.

14. David Bohm, quoted in *Brain/Mind Bulletin,* Volume 6, Number 1, 11/24/80.

SECTION IV–THE SERVANT PARABLES

1. Emmet Fox, *Make Your Life Worth While.* New York, Harper & Brothers, 1942, 1943, 1944, 1945, 1946, p. 167.

2. *In Parables,* pp. 25, 35.

3. *The Parables of Jesus,* p. 187, footnote.

4. Luke 21:34–36; 1 Thessalonians 5:6-8; 1 Corinthians 15:32–34; Thomas 28; The Odes of Solomon 38:10–15; Corpus Hermeticum, I, 27

5. *In Parables,* pp. 112–114.

6. Gerald H. Slusser, *From Jung to Jesus: Myth and Consciousness in the New Testament.* Atlanta: John Knox Press, 1986, pp. 114–115.

7. Philip J. King, *Amos, Hosea, Micah–An Archaeological Commentary.* Philadelphia: The Westminster Press, 1988, p. 119.

8. Jessie B. Rittenhouse, from *The Door of Dreams.* Boston: Houghton, Mifflin & Co.

9. *Gospel Light,* p. 286.
10. Ibid., pp. 280–283.
11. *In Parables,* pp. 89-90.
12. An ancient Jewish work, 1 Enoch, has a section (Chapter 63) dealing with "The hopeless end of the kings, rulers, and landlords." See *The Old Testament Pseudepigrapha,* edited by James H. Charlesworth, Vol. 1, p. 44. Published by Doubleday, 1983.
13. *Learn To Live,* pp. 143–144.

SECTION V–PARABLES OF FORGIVENESS

1. Will Campbell, quoted in *Atlanta Weekly,* April 19, 1981, article entitled, "Travels with Brother Will."
2. *The Gospel of Truth,* p. 128.
3. *Gospel Light,* p. 274.
4. *Jesus' Answer to God,* p. 162.
5. Edward F. Edinger, *The Bible and the Psyche: Individuation Symbolism in the Old Testament.* Toronto: Inner City Books, 1986, pp. 57–58.
6. *National Geographic Magazine,* Vol. 166, No. 5, November 1984, article entitled "Africa Adorned," by Angela Fisher, p. 600. Fisher has also written a book with the same title, published by Harry N. Abrams in New York.
7. For some excellent discussion questions relevant to this parable, see Walter Wink, *Transforming Bible Study.* Nashville, Abingdon Press, 1980, pp. 146–147.
8. John A. Sanford, *The Kingdom Within.* New York: Paulist Press, 1970, p. 153.
9. *The Sermon on the Mount,* p. 186. Emphasis is in the original.
10. *Learn To Live,* p. 227.
11. *In Parables,* p. 69.
12. Ibid. pp. 59–60. Crossan gives additional reasons supporting this conclusion.
13. Ibid. p. 66.

SECTION VI–OBSTACLES ON THE PATH

1. Swami Prabhavananda and Frederick Manchester, *The Upanishads–Breath of the Eternal*. New York: Mentor Books, 1948, p. 27.
2. *Learn To Live*, p. 154.
3. *The Parables of Jesus*, p. 170.
4. *The Archetypes and the Collective Unconscious*, pp. 109–110.
5. *The Interpreter's Dictionary of the Bible*, article on "Flora" by M. Zohary. Nashville: The Abingdon Press, 1962, Volume II, pp. 286–287.
6. *Jesus' Answer to God*, p. 184.

SECTION VII–THE CONSUMMATION

1. John Dominic Crossan, *Cliffs of Fall–Paradox and Polyvalence in the Parables of Jesus*. New York: The Seabury Press, 1980, p. 49.
2. Krister Stendahl, *Meanings: The Bible as Document and as Guide*. Philadelphia: Fortress Press, 1984, p. 236.
3. *The Archetypes and the Collective Unconscious*, pp. 177–178.
4. *The Gospel of Truth*, p. 104.
5. Charles Fillmore, *The Revealing Word*. Lee's Summit: Unity School of Christianity, 1959, p. 162.
6. Denise L. Carmody, *The Oldest God–Archaic Religion Yesterday and Today*. Nashville: Abingdon Press, 1981, pp. 47–48.
7. Paul Ricoeur, *Essays on Biblical Interpretation*. Philadelphia: Fortress Press, 1980, pp. 119–154.
8. *Aion*, pp. 170–171. Doctor Jung reviews the work of the alchemist Gerhard Dorn with respect to the image of the living stone.
9. Exodus 33:21; Deuteronomy 32:4, 18, 31; 2 Samuel 22:2–3; Psalm 18:2, 31; 27:5; 28:1; 40:2; 61:2; 62:2, 6–7; 71:3; 78:35; 89:26; 92:15; 94:22; 95:1; Isaiah 17:10; 28:16–18; 51:1; Daniel 2:34–35
10. *The Sermon on the Mount*, pp. 152–153.
11. *Aion*, p. 203.

12. *The Bible and the Psyche,* p. 58.

13. James H. Charlesworth, ed., *The Old Testament Pseudepigrapha,* Volume 1, translation of "Apocalypse of Sedrach" by S. Agourides, 1983, p. 610. Since the Apocalypse of Sedrach is written in Greek, and Jesus' parable foils it, it suggests the possibility that Jesus—unlike his other (Aramaic language) parables—gave the parable of the prodigal son in Greek.

14. The parable's outcome was even more startling to Jesus' hearers. For in favoring the younger son, it contradicts the crass favoritism that eastern men generally show toward their *first-born* sons. See *Gospel Light, op. cit.,* pp. 275–277.

15. Carl G. Jung, *Psychology and Religion: West and East.* Princeton: Princeton University Press, 1958, p. 276. Also see *The Bible and the Psyche, op. cit.,* p. 68.

16. Ibid., p. 281.

17. F.W. Rawson, *Life Understood.* London: The Society for Spreading the Knowledge of True Prayer, 1912, p. 91.